Declutter Your Life:

Simple Decluttering Strategies on How to Declutter and Organize your Life to Free Yourself from Worry and Enjoy Stress-Free Living

Madeline Crawford

© **Copyright 2019 by Madeline Crawford - All rights reserved.**

The contents of this book may not be reproduced, duplicated, or transmitted without direct written permission from the author.

Under no circumstances will any legal responsibility or blame be held against the publisher for any reparation, damages, or monetary loss due to the information herein, either directly or indirectly.

Legal Notice:

This book is copyright protected; it is only for personal use. You cannot amend, distribute, sell, use, quote, or paraphrase any part of the content within this book without the consent of the author.

Disclaimer Notice:

Please note the information contained within this document is for educational and entertainment purposes only. Every attempt has been made to provide accurate, up to date, and completely reliable information. No warranties of any kind are expressed or implied. Readers acknowledge that the author is not engaging in the rendering of legal, financial, medical, or professional advice. The content of this book has been derived from various sources. Please consult a licensed professional before attempting any techniques outlined in this book.

By reading this document, the reader agrees that under no circumstances is the author responsible for any losses, direct or indirect, which are incurred as a result of the use of the information contained within this document, including, but not limited to, —errors, omissions, or inaccuracies.

Table of Contents

Introduction

Chapter 1: Declutter Your Life - The Starting Point

Chapter 2: Proper Mindset When Decluttering Your Life

Chapter 3: Planning Your Time

Chapter 4: Organizing Family Activities

Chapter 5: Achieving a Clutter-Free Home

Chapter 6: Organizing Your Finances

Chapter 7: Decluttering with Others in Your Life

Chapter 8: Freeing Your Mind from Worry, Anxiety, and Stress

Chapter 9: Decluttering in the Workplace

Chapter 10: Freeing Yourself from Digital Distractions and Clutter

Chapter 11: The Simple Lifestyle

Bonus Chapter: Planning Family Recreational Activities

Conclusion

References

Introduction:

We often relate clutter mainly to material things. We see clothing placed over the dresser, on top of the treadmill, and covering other available surfaces in the bedroom. Then we see magazines and books scattered across the coffee table and extra dishes stacked on the counter.

In truth, clutter can also be a social, emotional, and mental issue. The demands we face every day can lead to an increase in stress at a point in our lives.

Various aspects of our lives can become overwhelming, leading to struggles from financial mismanagement to home clutter to messy schedules that seem to be impossible to get organized. You may need to address a different type of clutter if your mind is busy with various thoughts. Or are tired because of a full weekly schedule that prevents you from sleeping adequately.

If your goal is to declutter, it's crucial to keep in

mind that there are valid reasons that allow for the buildup of material things. It's in human nature to get disorganized from time to time. We are more likely to get disorganized during our busy lives, such as moving into a new house or being tied up in a big project at school or work.

The buildup will inevitably occur despite our best efforts to prevent clutter from happening, and this is entirely normal. When it comes to our degree of tolerance toward clutter, we all differ. You must always be diligent about picking up and staying organized because it's hard to declutter once your lack of order becomes notorious.

One of the main reasons for the difficulty of decluttering is that we find it hard to let go of things. The way hoarders feel when they give away objects with which they have formed an attachment is similar to the feeling of physical pain. Studies have shown that giving others our prized possessions activated the same area in our brain that recognizes pain. In other words, giving things away literally hurts. We become more attached to an object as we spend more time with it.

Being disorganized or cluttered is a normal part of life, while hoarding is a physiological disorder. In non-hoarders, the neurological reaction to giving things away is much less intense than that of hoarders. The response is still present, though, so it's worth pointing out.

Having this in the back of your mind will make it easier for you to get rid of things. You will find yourself in situations where you want to keep something because you feel attached to it. In these instances, you should assess to determine the validity of your attachment by asking yourself whether you are indeed connected to it or if you are considering the pain that comes with losing that item.

There is a theory that asserts that clutter is the symptom of indecisiveness. Struggling with indecision can be the result of growing up in a home where no item was ever discarded or having difficulties revolving around making the right choice. Regardless of its origin, your indecision may make it very difficult for you to figure out whether to keep an object or not. You instead tend to forego that decision by merely holding on to that object, thereby surpassing making a decision altogether.

When it comes to decluttering, the reason for keeping an item is more important than the object itself.

In later chapters, we will be discussing this in more detail and providing solutions.

The famous duo known as "The Minimalists" says that the reason for our clutter is more important than how we clutter. They associate clutter with a consumerist mindset which has become a feature of modern society. When decluttering, it helps to understand the basics of minimalism as well as its practice to distinguish between necessary and unnecessary items.

There is a saying by Albert Einstein that goes as follows: "If a cluttered desk is a sign of a cluttered mind, of what, then, is an empty desk a sign?"

This quote is an intriguing point that several people have taken to heart. Most people believe very creative and highly intelligent individuals work from messy desks or reside in messy houses.

There's some truth in the great Einstein's statement1 showed that people found it easier to come up with solutions to a creative challenge when they were in a messy area than in an organized one. A lot of people jokingly use this to justify messy workplaces, but as with most things in life, there's more underneath the surface.

In a different study,2). Only 47 percent of those participants that were in the disorganized room donated, while 87 percent of people that were in the cleanroom donated. The final part of the experiment involved offering each participant the choice of candy or an apple on their way out. Can you guess who chose the apple? The people from the cleanroom were more than three times as likely to opt for a healthy choice.

So, what have we learned from these studies? While disorderliness increases your creative capabilities, cleanliness encourages you to make the right decisions. Other conclusions can be drawn from different results. A study found that interested and curious individuals and people with many interests were more likely to be disorganized. In reality, these results may have more to do with the type of people involved in the study than the state of their surroundings.

Every one of us has an optimum work environment. For some people, this can be a clear desk with a laptop, a pen, and a notepad. For other people, it is a kitchen table filled with a few printouts, some books, a couple of handouts, a laptop, a water bottle, and a cup of coffee. This setup goes beyond your home and your workspace. Some people feel good when everything around them is orderly and clean, while others may feel that decluttering every day is a bit excessive.

The most important thing you can do is find your best balance. This sweet spot also applies to your spouse if you have one. Doing this reduces stress. Take a second and think about your digital workspace. You make life easier for yourself by clearing your inbox and decluttering your browser tabs and your desktop. Doing this will force you back up old but essential files. You can even find things you thought you had lost, such as past articles in Pocket, or rediscover some old notes on Evernote. You can inject new energy into your life through digital decluttering.

I firmly believe material possessions do not equate to happiness. This belief made me try out the idea of minimalistic living. I wanted to see if I would obtain a less cluttered mind if I spent time in a less cluttered home.

I made decluttering every aspect of my life my priority and achieved my goals by getting rid of all the things I felt were unnecessary. Doing this reduced the number of my material possessions, which in turn helped me focus on my most valuable items.

Take a look below at the seven steps I followed to declutter my belongings:

- **Step 1**: I sorted my possessions into their appropriate categories, such as shoes, jewelry, clothes, cosmetics, books, electronics, bags, and so on.

- **Step 2**: I took out everything from one category so that I could have an idea of the number of items within the category as well as the category's size compared to others.

- **Step 3**: I got rid of any items that immediately seemed unnecessary.

- **Step 4**: I carefully worked my way through the remaining items, and I discarded anything I didn't need or the things I didn't love.

- **Step 5**: This was a tough call, and I needed to face it without unnecessary sentiments. I removed items in my "keep pile" after further consideration as to whether I loved them or not.

- **Step 6**: I organized the items I decided to keep.

- **Step** 7: I gave away the items that didn't make the "keep pile" to charity shops, friends, and recycling centers.

Clutter can be a significant energy drain or a severe waste of time for most people, as it makes it challenging to locate what they need. In extreme cases, clutter can be a cause of depression or even of obesity, especially when a life of consumption goes beyond just stuff. A cluttered house can cause health complications due to the accumulation of dust and mold, and clutter can cause fire hazards, especially in situations where a person is a hoarder. However, extreme cases are not very common.

Here is a bit of good news for you: decluttering can become more straightforward and less time consuming, producing little or no physical or emotional stress. Many lessons are learned while decluttering, and the sense of achievement and control that come at the end of the process can be a significant stress reliever.

By discarding unnecessary items, you may free up much-needed space at home. It is also helpful to declutter before you move to a new house. The decluttering strategies you are going to encounter in this comprehensive guide will assist you on your journey toward a clutter-free life.

In this book, you will find detailed solutions on how to declutter and simplify your life. These solutions also include organizing your activities, finances, and even your digital files, all aimed to help you live a decluttered, stress-free life.

Chapter 1: Declutter Your Life - The Starting Point

Chapter 1: Declutter Your Life - The Starting Point

There's a common misconception that clutter only relates to physical items. When we think of clutter, we visualize magazines and books scattered on the coffee table, clothes tossed in weird places, or extra dishes on the counter. The truth is that clutter can also manifest as a social, emotional, or mental issue.

You have a cluttered mind when it is filled with competing thoughts, and this can affect your sleep. You may also be exhausted after hectic weekly schedules. This issue certainly isn't physical clutter, but rather clutter in another form.

To accurately define clutter as what it is, you need to know what it is not. Clutter is not the same thing as dirt. Even the neatest housekeepers can have clutter accumulating on their desks and shelves.

Clutter and hoarding are two different things. Clutter is something that happens when you unintentionally collect items throughout your home or space. Hoarding, on the other hand, is the unhealthy process of holding on to unnecessary stuff. All that is needed to correct clutter is being committed to the organization, while hoarding may need external intervention to be fixed.

Clutter does not include collecting valuable items. My aunt collects ends and odds from around the world. Her house is full of collectibles, yet it doesn't feel cluttered, and this is because she displays them on shelves or in cabinets. Things aren't laying around in areas of frequent use such as kitchen counters or walkways.

The Origin of Clutter

You would look for and close off the source of a leak in the basement before you start collecting the water, right? With that in mind, let's familiarize ourselves with the way clutter forms before we begin to look at ways to get rid of it. When it comes to clutter, everyone living in a home contributes to its accumulation, especially the little ones. Kids drag home small items from their meals or parties, and they leave their toys out.

Like kids, adults also generate clutter. This clutter usually happens when we feel we're too busy to return an object to its rightful place. The result is leaving it anywhere that is convenient at that moment, like the dining table.

These items gradually accumulate, and in no time, a small pile becomes a sizeable one. Catalogs, junk mail, and magazine subscriptions are another means through which we gain clutter.

By recognizing the role you play in accumulating clutter, you are a step closer to reducing it. Failure to accept responsibilities is one of the things that hinders the decluttering process at home. Families spend their time blaming one another for the clutter instead of taking the fact that everyone plays a role, then moving forward toward a solution.

Definition of "Clutter" and "Decluttering"

The words "decluttering" and "clutter" often appear with one another, but what do they mean? It's essential to know the meaning of these terms, as they form the basis of the problem this book aims to solve.

My idea of physical clutter is items that do the following:

- make your space messy or disordered;
- are unnecessary and don't contribute to your happiness
- they keep postponing your decision on what to do with them.

In my opinion, clutter is a symptom, not a cause; it is a symptom of the inability to make the right decisions (or any decisions for that matter) concerning the items in your space. There are many reasons for this. You may find it hard because it's an emotional decision, or you may have a hectic schedule and finding it hard to find the time needed to put things in order.

Decluttering is the process by which you determine whether items in your space are clutter, and you decide to put the necessary things in the right place. By helping you understand the reason there's clutter in the first place, decluttering allows you to make the permanent changes required. Hoarding Disorders UK have a useful measure of information on clutter found on their website. The image scale on the site helps viewers determine the condition of their space by picking the picture in the sequence that closely resembles the situations in their rooms. According to Hoarding Disorders UK, having things around you might reach a point where it starts to encroach on other people's lives to the point where you might have to seek help for your hoarding problem When it comes to clutter, the most critical aspect is how you feel about your space. We all have different ideas of what we consider to be clutter. For some people, something like a few clothes on a chair makes them feel like their home is cluttered. For some, they begin to feel their space is cluttered when piled-up objects start to limit their movements within the house.

One thing people who want to declutter have in common is the overwhelming feeling that comes from cluttered space. Ideally, your home should be a place that reduces your stress levels - a place where you can breathe easily. Your workspace should be a location where you feel productive, efficient, and in control (to a certain degree).

Importance of Decluttering Your Life

There are many benefits to decluttering than meets the eye; it has significant positive effects on your mind, body, and the world at large. Hearing this may be the push you need to get started. Read on and prime yourself for decluttering.

1. **Purifies the air around you.** Clutter attracts dust, and this reduces the purity of the air you breathe in. Few things do as much good for your body and mind as some spring (or summer, fall, or winter) cleaning. It purifies the air around you.

2. **Mind sharpening.** A Princeton University study found that the brain's

ability to focus improves as you declutter your living and working spaces3. In simple terms, by having fewer things to divert your attention to, such as clutter, you have a more productive mind for concentrating on the task at hand.

3. **Eliminates negative energy**. A common place to find clutter is in a room behind closed doors. The reason is this room is something no one wants to see, yet everyone in the house knows it is there. It becomes taboo to talk about this spare room. Here's the thing - everything gives off either positive or negative energy. The question is, which one do you want more?

4. **It makes room for promising opportunities**. Everyone wants better things coming in their lives, but these things are blocked by some of the old stuff we won't do away with. For example, you would love to bring in new clients for your

business, but your workspace is filled with paper, garbage, and old files. New clients can't come if the old stuff remains there.

5. **It makes you money**. Who doesn't want to have more money? The money you so deserve is probably right in front of you in the form of the heap of stuff in your garage, spare room, or attic. By selling these things, you could make enough money to take a friend out for dinner, take a short vacation, pay off a little debt, open a savings account, or pay for anything else you can imagine.

6. **Mindful purchasing**. When we make purchases, it is usually on a whim. This action is a waste of hard-earned money because we aren't considering whether we need or like such items. By decluttering, we develop a mindset that directs us to make better decisions when it comes to purchasing things.

7. **Money saved from unnecessary and**

frivolous purchases. You can save a lot of money by limiting your purchases to only the items you feel are necessary. You'll be surprised to find out that the group of items you spend the most money on can be clothing. By reducing your clothes shopping, you will have more money in your pocket to do the things you love.

8. **Creativity stimulation**. Removing excess clutter from your space stimulates your creativity. It also calms your mind, and this makes it easier for you to create beautiful works. Give your creativity a boost by tidying your environment.

9. **Save time by being able to find things more easily**. Your time is precious, and it probably shouldn't be spent hunting through pile after pile of stuff just to find any item you are looking for. By reducing your possessions, you can find things faster and spend less time looking for them. This approach is better

than rooting through hangers of clothes or diving into a mountain of handbags just to find a specific one.

10. **Space is saved from owning less.** The amount of storage space you need increases with the number of materials you possess. You may discover you need about half of your space after decluttering. This discovery may prompt you to get a smaller apartment. This move would be more economical than your current area, which may be bigger than what you need.

11. **Happier outlook.** You feel more satisfied when you surround yourself with items that are precious to you. Undesirable items will no longer cover your favorite things or lodged in strange places like the bottom of the drawer or behind the cupboard. Your favorite items do not need to be reserved for only special occasions. They can and should be out in the open all the time for you to see and

use freely. This approach will most certainly make you a happier person.

12. **Quicker and more accessible to clean and tidy**. It is much easier to clean a house with few possessions than it is to clean one filled with clutter. Every item has a place, and it is best if you know exactly where to find everything. You can only achieve this by reducing the number of your possessions. Your mind will be less cluttered once your living space is tidier.

13. **More freedom**. A sense of freedom and lightness awaits you when you place greater importance on experiences than materials and let go of material possessions. You can get addicted to the wonderful sense of freedom that comes with being rid of suffocating and unnecessary materials. By detaching yourself from possessions, you can shift your focus to better things like experiences and people.

14. **Promotes relaxation**. Your stress levels at home are at their peak when you are dealing with belongings. By reducing the amount of time spent dealing with your stuff, you can significantly reduce your stress levels. Applying this habit also helps you to become a calmer individual.

15. **Move forward already**. That box containing cards, letters, trinkets, and so on from your ex-boyfriend or ex-girlfriend is only going to hold you back. Face it - you got hurt and they aren't coming back so why do you keep holding on to those things? Let it go! Accept it, and move on with your life. You must love tormenting yourself if you choose to keep reading those old letters, and it's awful for your mental health, so you should stop doing so.

16. **You are helping others**. You don't have to throw out your unnecessary items, because they may be useful to someone else. Make sure to think about

whether the things you are considering throwing away can be donated to a business or thrift store to help out someone else and prevent waste.

17. **Get the monkey off your back**. This monkey goes by a familiar name: clutter. He sits on your back, and he pokes you very hard from time to time. As you have imagined, he is very annoying. He times his pokes at the exact moment you walk by the garage and other places that have accumulated stuff. As if poking you wasn't infuriating enough, he laughs hysterically at you, because he knows you are not going to do a thing about that mess. Haven't you had enough of him? His taunts only raise your stress levels. Since he weighs a ton, he makes your steps heavier than they should be. Get rid of him so that you can be light on your feet.

Decluttering Myths Debunked

Decluttering could be done in more than one way and leads to organizing space. Practices and methods of decluttering that work for one person might not work for another without some modifications. And just like everything, decluttering also has its myth. Below is a list of popular decluttering myths.

Myth #1: You must be organized every day of the week.

The truth: No matter how organized you are, the gathering of clutter (no matter how little) is inevitable in life.

At times, you may need to rest instead of cleaning up because you have had a long and stressful day. It's okay. Give yourself a little break and take care of your cleaning chores the following day. You would most likely do a more efficient job organizing with your batteries recharged.

Having a routine and schedule is the key that allows you to maintain a neat home without worrying about decluttering or feeling burnt out. Impossibly high standards of organization would only cause disappointment and frustration.

Myth #2: Decluttering only needs to be done once in a while.

The truth: The process of decluttering is an ongoing and regular process.

You would be free from the disorganized and burdensome feeling associated with living in a cluttered home if you must invest time in a major decluttering project. Although working to reduce the clutter is an excellent first step. A focused effort to declutter once a year isn't enough.

A schedule for regular decluttering is the only way of consistently having a neat home and organized life. Endeavor to set time for this task weekly. Give a little more time to your cleaning and decluttering tasks once regularly.

Myth #3: Having an empty space is a bad thing.

The truth: At times, it is about what is not present when it comes to what a room looks like to you.

Maybe it is the negative meaning of the word

'empty' which shows an empty space as a bad thing.

The term "negative space" from the art world has been borrowed by some interior decorators to describe spaces in the home intentionally unoccupied by furniture or even artwork on the walls. It is no wonder the concept gets a bad reputation as "negative" is attached to its name.

Decluttering does not only entail removing junk and cleaning up. It could also include intentionally keeping space or spaces empty while making decorating choices. That serves a few objectives.

First, a less occupied space could induce calm and not be too much for our brains. Our attention could also be drawn to other items as well as features present in the room, which becomes more pronounced in empty spaces.

"Clutter" does not only indicate piles of useless things. It could also be putting too many things on the walls or corners. The island and table are more pronounced due to the intentional use of empty space.

Myth #4: A messy individual is unable to change their poor organization habits.

The truth: This is a decluttering myth that we can refer to as nonsense.

Being a well-organized individual is not a character or a trait; it is actually a skill. And like every skill, organizational skills can be learned, and it can build up over time depending on the individual's patience and will to build the capability.

If you consider figurative expressions like "you can't teach an old dog new tricks," or "a leopard can't change its spots," it appears that it might be a bit difficult to get an older person to become neat all of a sudden.

However, if you consider an expression like "if you're not learning you're not living," and many more words of wisdom concerning learning, it is possible for positive change.

Myth #5: The way to go is to live a minimalist lifestyle.

The truth: It does not apply to everyone.

Many people have been taught to live with fewer things, with media articles advising to re-examine our consumerist inclination. However, not everyone sees enjoyment as an include extreme and sudden downsizing to live in a small shipping container, micro condo, or tiny home.

Having more things not needed by you does not make you worse than someone practicing the minimalist lifestyle. It all boils down to personal preference.

Ensure that you do not buy too many things which leads to you drowning in clutter. Buy the things you need only, and not just the item you want, or things you think you need. There is a saying which thus "Own your things, don't let your things own you."

Myth #6: You can remain organized without some extra help.

The truth: Many great organization helpers exist all over the world. Make proper use of them.

The variation of these common decluttering myths is that you are capable of keeping a neat home without spending money on storage systems as well as a quality organization.

Correct, it can be done, but why not make it easier for yourself?

There are lots of wonderful products available (such as bed surrounds and closet organizers) which are explicitly designed to increase storage space and prevent time-wasting. These tools make it less challenging to stay organized.

Although these useful tools do not do all the work in keeping you organized, they make it easier for you to stay organized. There are various great products which can help you to stay organized with little effort, take advantage of it.

Myth #7: It is manageable to live with clutter.

The truth: Indeed, you can technically live a chaotic life and get used to the clutter surrounding you. However, the

longer you leave your clutter, the more your life becomes unmanageable.

Think about the time wasted every day when searching for items in a disorganized office or home. In addition to the causes of time-wasting clutter, it can also lead to poor sleeping habits and stress, as well as other medical problems.

Step-by-Step Strategy on How to Declutter Your Life and Lower Stress Levels

Deciding to declutter your home is not an easy task, and its difficulty can sometimes make it unappealing to attempt. Decluttering is no different from other things in life in that the hardest part is getting started. Listed below are reliable decluttering tips that will aid you as you begin to regain control of your space by clearing clutter.

Step 1: Set goals. Having a plan before you begin an activity goes a long way in making the whole process easier for you. Specific goals will help to tackle decluttering, regardless of the amount of clutter you have ahead of you. Below are some of the things you should consider before deciding to declutter your home:

- Make physical notes or draw up a map showing clutter within the house.

- Give each room a grade based on the clutter within that space. For example, you can use a scale of 1-3 with 3 being highest; a messy closet or room would be a 3. This grading system helps you prioritize your time.

- Visualize your goal (in this case, your dream room) before you begin. Take note of its details, use, and the placement of your possessions. Let your vision direct your decluttering efforts. If you come across a lovely picture online or in a magazine, try to reproduce the feel of it in your own space. The more specific your vision, the higher your level of motivation.

- Schedule deadlines for the completion of each phase of your cleanup. To avoid frustration, make your deadlines attainable. Decluttering can be fun if you challenge yourself.

- To complement your completion dates, have plans to tackle the specific areas with the highest amount of clutter, like a garage or basement. These areas may require more than a couple of hours to declutter.

Step 2: Create a sorting system. A sorting system is necessary for your decluttering to be effective. You can come up with your own method, or you can use the "Three-Box Method," which happens to be one of the most organizational strategies. What this method does is it puts you in a situation whereby you must make a single decision on the fate of every single item in your possession.

Get three boxes or storage bins, and label them as detailed using the guide below:

- **"Keep" box.** You empty this box when you complete a space. The items from this box should go to designated locations in your home. You should store them neatly in a drawer or container, and label them if you so desire.

- **"Get rid of" box.** As with the previous box, empty this one when you are done with the area. Put any items you want to sell or give away into this box. If you don't have a storage space, keep them in the vehicle you plan on using to transport them to a store. They can also temporarily go in the attic or garage.

- **"Put in storage" box.** Put the contents of this box in storage containers, label the containers or place an inventory sheet on them, and arrange them neatly in your storage area.

Step 3: Get mentally prepared. Decluttering is a time-consuming process, and accepting this fact will make your journey easier. The clutter you are clearing didn't appear overnight, so it can't be handled in an instant. Always keep this in mind: small steps in the proper direction still count as steps in the appropriate direction. You will gradually move toward your objectives.

- **Until you are done decluttering, try not to bring new things into your home.** You do not want to add to your considerable workload by bringing home new items.

- **Ask yourself the right questions.** You need to ask yourself this when you come across an item while decluttering: Does this spark joy? This practical question has its downsides. For most people, it can be a trap, because they find ways to justify keeping items that make them happy, even if they rarely use them.

  A practical and straightforward mantra to decide on what things to give up or keep is "use it, cherish it, or let it go". Do you use it frequently? Do you cherish it, or does it help to make your life better in a way (such as photographs, souvenirs, or artwork)? If your answers in response to all these questions are negative, then that item should not go in the keep pile.

- **Keep your vision in mind and follow through with it.** Always have the image of your desired room in mind as you declutter. When you find yourself struggling with decisions on your possessions, ask yourself these two questions:

    o What's presently in the space that would take me away from my vision?

    o What's in my space right now that will bring the room closer to my vision?

- **If the decluttering becomes difficult, continue to persevere by using your motto.** Decision fatigue is going to set in at some point, and that's okay. Instead of giving up, use a mantra. Here are some effective mantras to keep you going when things get tough and to remind you why you're decluttering:

    o If you keep too much, you can't find what's essential.

- Your desk is a work surface, not a storage area.

- Your bed is a space for sleeping, not a dirty clothes hamper.

- Your nightstand is home to your lamp and a couple of books; it's not a medicine cabinet.

Step 4: Start sorting

- **Tackle one room or one space at a time.** It's most effective to start with the place that is bothering you the most, whether it's the junk drawer, garage, bedroom closet, or kitchen. By taking on the room that causes the most significant spike in your stress levels and makes you want to run away, you build up the motivation and momentum needed to follow the task through to the end. You can also achieve the same effect by primarily working on the space that affects your daily life the most.

- **Start with what you can see.** You've

marked your problem area, so now you should gradually begin decluttering by working on the items you can see. These are visible surfaces like desktops, tables, floor space, or the tops of dressers. After handling these, you can move on to deeper regions, like cabinets and drawers.

- **Don't forget to focus on the big stuff, too.** It's easy to ignore the big stuff when you are faced with little things like the items scattered on the bookshelf. Big things can create even more chaos than the small stuff. Furniture placement, for example, can be a form of visual clutter and may make long-term organization difficult.

  If you have too many unused large toys or furniture in a single room, you should move these items out. You can give yourself a motivation boost by reorganizing your space. Clutter also ruins your sleep, and nobody wants that.

- **Declutter one item at a time.** Clutter

is the result of deferred decision making, so it is better to handle things one at a time to make reasonable progress.

- **Turn sentimental items into stories.** Sentimental items can be tough to part with. However, with a simple strategy, you can make what is usually a tough decision a bit easier. Simply take a picture of the item, and write an accompanying story about its history and significance. This picture and its emotional message are more precious than an item you no longer use. You also need to consider the fact that the person who gave you such an item wouldn't want it being a burden to you.

- **Give everything a home.** Finding a specific space for each item goes a long way in ensuring clutter doesn't accumulate again. If you are unable to allocate a designated area for an object, continue reducing your things until you find one.

- **Seek assistance from an expert.** You can always reach out to a professional organizer if you have trouble decluttering. Obtaining expert advice during the decluttering and organizational process will immensely increase your chances of getting the job done. You can also schedule a pickup when you have figured out the items you will want to store.

Step 5: Get rid of the clutter. You have a couple of options when it comes to disposing of the items in the "get rid of it" box.

- **Recycle.** Recyclable paper, glass, and plastics can go in the recycling bin if you have curbside pickup. If not, your recyclables should go into a bag so that you can take them to the closest recycling center to you.

  A lot of electronic gadgets should be recycled. There are over 1,890 EcoATM recycling kiosks in 42 states. These kiosks give you cash from your old electronics. Check prices for your old devices, and use the ecoATM locator to find the nearest one to you.

- **Donate or freecycle.** It is refreshing to know your unwanted item will be transferred to a new home. Shoes, clothes, and other household pieces in proper form can be given as donations to a local charity of your choice as long you follow the charity's donation guidelines.

  You also have the option of making a post on freecycle.org. You can post the things you want to dispose of and people, can come and pick up the items. What you regard as trash might be very valuable to someone else.

- **Have a garage sale.** You can make money off your clutter if you are up to the challenge. You can do this by having a garage sale. Check if your neighborhood or homeowner's association has a garage sale date set aside. You should start your decluttering early so that you have enough items to display at the sale. By having a lot of goods shown, you will have more foot traffic, and this usually results in more sales.

- **Rent a dumpster.** This option is a very affordable and stress-free one for those who have a lot of items to get rid of. It can also be used by people who want to dispose of large household items. If you rent a dumpster, your only task is to fill their vehicle up with your unwanted items. They will haul it away when you are done. It's that simple!

Your Quick Start Action Step:

1. Look around your house and assess the level of disorganization.
2. Think of the areas in your house that need to be organized.
3. Evaluate your life and list areas that need to be organized.
4. Picture how those places in your house and areas in your life will look like after you organize.
5. Write down the benefits you'll gain

after you organize.

Chapter 2: Proper Mindset when Decluttering Your Life

Chapter 2: Proper Mindset When Decluttering Your Life

Your frame of mind encompasses the entirety of your knowledge. These include your values and opinions about life and your role in it. It helps you sort through every piece of information you come across and determine what is useful and what is not. Hence, it influences the way you take in knowledge as well as respond to it.

More often than not, having the proper mindset for the choices you make is the most significant factor. Cultivating the appropriate mindset is essential to excel in anything at all. Subsequently, you create the values that are most beneficial for your purpose or ambition. This system of belief is therefore referred to as your mindset.

We will assume that an abundant mindset will portray authenticity and help you. The arrangement has to be something like this:

- Identify the most helpful beliefs and values.

- Determine those beliefs that agree with (a possible) reality.

It is good that you channel your mindset into something productive; this explains why your beliefs and values don't have to portray your present situation. However, the reality that you hold to be valid must be achievable. It is like a catch-22, but not exactly.

If you think you're well-coordinated, you will act accordingly. If you believe you wish to be a well-organized person, you must act equally accordingly - like an unorganized person.

The idea of embracing a seemingly difficult belief is impressive, because it affects your mindset, and ultimately, how you act, in a positive way. It allows growth. If you desire to do anything remarkable at all, you must then cultivate the habit of following through.

This approach is where most of us falter because acting on it is daunting. It will cost you the habit of persistence necessary to carry out your lifestyle goals. You also need to be daring enough to set giant, intimidating goals and then tell those who you can share it with that you will achieve these goals.

You must have the courage to claim a piece of the pie for yourself. Additionally, it takes endurance and persistence - a lot of it. At the same time, a great deal of hard work is required before you will ever benefit from the time and effort you may have invested. This action runs the risk of becoming extremely frustrating, but in the end, it could provide lasting benefits.

You may be wondering what the way out is. It is forming the habit of endurance better than anyone else around you and enjoying the grueling work, regardless of what anyone else advises. This outlook becomes a positive mindset to achieve your personal goal.

Any gainful course requires endurance, but when the goal is achieved, the means are justified.

What makes having the right mindset so important?

If you are truly determined to be successful in

any of your endeavors, then you definitely must learn how to develop the right mindset for the reasons that are mentioned below.

1. **It is building a healthy self-esteem.** To achieve anything meaningful, a person must first be confident of the fact that he can accomplish it, whether everybody agrees or not. Self-esteem emanates from an inner conversation that determines what price we place on our worth, as well as how we see ourselves. Also, it forms the general idea we have of ourselves.

   A positive and strong mindset is vital in developing healthy self-esteem. It affects our everyday self-talk and reinforces the feelings, beliefs, and attitudes that we hold dear to us. So, manage your state of mind by planting seeds of inspiration and positivity instead of criticizing and doubting yourself

2. **Creating a success perspective.** When success is involved, several aspects are more critical to reaching this

perspective. The importance attached to events and situations has an intense effect on how you view things, such as, for instance, seeing a glass as either half empty or half full. In life, nothing has an inherent meaning except that which is given to it.

The truth is, your state of mind has absolutely everything to do with your perception of life. The beliefs formed early in life, your manner of approach, and your prejudices automatically influence your response to details as well as how you view the world around you. Keeping a positive outlook on life increases the chances of creating a success perspective and of obtaining lasting success.

3. **You are channeling your drive.** Drive refers to a stubborn resolve to accomplish a vital objective. It involves the process of creating a mental picture of success and maintaining a constant effort over time.

When the drive is absent, it will be almost impossible to achieve most objectives.

Your mindset is vital to your drive. When channeled and focused on a lasting purpose, you can propel yourself toward above your present status. It also means that you move beyond the settled method of doing things that requires little effort and yield only barely acceptable results.

Those who have passion are self-motivated and do their best to achieve more. These people do not laze around complaining about their circumstances or give excuses; instead, they focus on improving their situation.

4. **Being faced with adversity.** It doesn't matter what you are out to accomplish; you will experience some level of trouble and hardships on the road to success. Nevertheless, if you wish to survive the difficulties, you will learn to develop resistance and deal with each challenge with everything you've got.

It is at this juncture that your mindset comes to play. Adversity tries one's courage to the crux. After being faced with tremendous difficulty, an individual might feel like he or she has every reason to throw in the towel. To such people, that might appear to be the easiest way out. Nonetheless, the ability to pass through fire and be battered but not defeated is a genuine proof of a resilient mindset.

5. **Accomplishing the fundamental objectives.** Goal-setting is a many-sided process, with accomplishment being the most palpable gauge for success. However, in the absence of the right mindset, you may end up not making it to that point. Accomplishing a target requires a better-than-average desire to achieve something.

Mindset is the point where your resiliencies are being put to the test. Mental toughness is what determines the likelihood of someone pushing beyond the surface to succeed despite the hardships being faced or merely succumbing to defeat. It is one of the many parts of practicing courage, sustaining effort over a long period, and engaging in internal monologues to move past through each critical stage before achieving the desired goal in the end.

How to Cultivate the Right Mindset While Decluttering

1. **Invest time in developing a standard for your vision and drive.** Vision does not exist where it is not first seen. Go beyond your comfort zone. Immerse yourself in and savor the taste of what you desire to achieve from decluttering your life. After you have done that, go ahead and ask yourself why it means so much to you. Discover the things that excite you.

   The vision you have is centered on you and your needs, and it must be entire, lucid, and brutally honest. Most often, people are ambiguous about their goals; all they have is an unclear vision of what they desire. Try to take a breather from the daily rollercoaster. Get yourself a notebook, find a serene environment, and write down the following: first is what you desire to achieve. Next is how you'll be able to track your achievements, and finally when you know that you have accomplished your goal(s).

Put everything into writing. Your mind would usually do what you will it to do. However, to reach a target, you must be clear about your mission. For this reason, begin writing your decluttering vision in complete detail.

2. **Believe you'll succeed.** The way we act is in keeping what we hold to be true. If you have a mindset of success, then you will be more likely to take steps that bring you closer to your target. You consider the possible options in the quest for the most promising way forward. You continue

despite hindrances and challenges because you have the confidence that you will scale through and remain on the road to success.

Those who learned to develop a positive mental framework ultimately leads to a productive approach to life's challenges, while those who don't may eventually give up.

If you have the opinion that you will do well where decluttering your life is involved, then you are, in essence, instructing your brain to accomplish it. You direct your attention towards the possibilities and the key that will help you to advance. Conversely, if you believe that you can't successfully declutter your life, you train your brain to look for reasons why you cannot achieve it.

Beliefs influence how we behave. We can hold on to beliefs that move us toward our target rather than those that prevent us from achieving them.

3. **Conquer one setback at a time.** We tend to mentally rush to the finish line when we get attached to the outcome. In this frame of mind, we put a high demand on ourselves to succeed. We become preoccupied with all the hindrances we may be faced with, and we do not embrace progressive advancement and expansion. All we want is to fast forward to the benefits of success.

We won't successfully take care of ten challenges at a go. Our minds are not capable of choosing where to channel our awareness. Our focus becomes dispersed, and our positive energy dissolves.

We can, however, conquer one room at a time. We are capable of evaluating each room systematically from all perspectives. Finally, we can create a stratagem to declutter in a manner that has a higher possibility of yielding success.

We should devote to a method and forge ahead. Simplifying the target and focusing exclusively on the next room or aspect of our life can be accomplished. The mindset yields sustained action, which contributes to a substantial advancement over time.

4. **Fortify your motivation continually.** Most of the time, you are aware of precisely what you want; however, after enduring the "go-get-it" syndrome for a period, you may begin to lose drive. This stage is when you reduce your pace and likely give up. Many times, you may be required to go beyond yourself to bring out the best. Meditate on these questions: who is influenced by my dream, and who is likely to benefit from it?

Think about those you loved. In what way are they likely to be affected a year after your dream is fulfilled? How about two years afterward? You are becoming more powerful, the benefits your family and friends enjoy are starting to grow, and your influence on the society around you multiplies. Imagine how it all amasses after five years or ten years. Fixate your mind on the goal, and experience the rush of excitement that will engulf you. Go back to this visualization process every time you need to renew your inspiration.

5. **Your sole competition should be you.** Prototyping the mindset, stratagem, and dealings of those who have already achieved what you are chasing after is precious. By modeling, you can avoid unnecessary errors committed by other people on their way to successful decluttering. You can find out a reliable plan that hastens the advancement to your goals.

While the process of acquiring knowledge from others improves your growth, mentally contending with them results in harmful repercussions. When you compare ourselves to others, you set your sights on more successful people. This attitude causes you to feel like you are not enough and second-guess your capabilities.

When you change your standards and contend only with yourself, you move faster on your way to a productive decluttering. You will become less affected by what others are engaging in. All you are trying to do is be better than you were yesterday. You are only concerned about making your home and life adequately planned, so you should evaluate your success solely on your personal targets for decluttering.

6. **Be proactive.** You must be active and ready to take the bull by the horns if you want to reduce clutter. Proactivity helps you to be in charge of your life rather than sit by the sidelines, watching it get filled with junk.

If you desire success in decluttering your life, you must be capable of making difficult choices to ensure your home and life are in order. If you are proactive, then ultimately, you will be pro-growth; as a result, you have made the most crucial decision to declutter successfully.

7. **Do not lose your sense of humor.** Decluttering can be a turbulent and overwhelming process that leaves you worn out and exhilarated at the same time. The secret to surviving this experience while at the same time maintaining sanity lies in your ability to be humorous and able to laugh at your errors.

If you allow each obstacle to drag you down, you will be rid of your sense of drive and the ability to function. Be open to each challenge as a fundamental aspect of the process; be grateful for how it provides you with another avenue to learn without shifting your focus.

Having the proper frame of mind is an extraordinary job. You may obtain counsel and assistance, but developing the right mindset leads you to success. Only bear in mind that starting decluttering requires hard work, but the benefits are tremendous and worth the effort.

Your Quick Start Action Step:

1. Write down ten reasons why you think you won't be able to declutter your home and life successfully.

2. Then write down at most two ways to combat each of the ten reasons listed in the first point.

3. Be ready to apply one of those two ways per problem when you begin to declutter, and the reasons in the first bullet start appearing.

Chapter 3: Planning Your Time

Chapter 3: Planning Your Time

Time organization refers to managing time optimally such that the right proportion of time is assigned to the correct activity. Effective time organization permits individuals to allocate a definite time gap to events according to their level of importance.

Even though everybody has the same 24 hours, time tends to be wasted as a result of mismanagement and lack of planning. Time organization refers to making the full use of time; after all, time is always limited.

Know which of the projects before you are most vital and the quantity of time you should assign to each. Ask yourself which work should be done first and which should be done later. This section of the book will help you deal with this challenge.

Below is detailed what makes managing your time important (in association with decluttering):

1. **Time organization helps you keep time and be disciplined.** You train yourself to work when it is necessary due to proper time organization. To make the maximum use of time, you must write a daily task plan or a to-do list each day. Based on the order of importance and urgency to meet up with the time allotted to each task, you should then try to make a list of activities required for that day.

   A to-do list will set you on track at your place of work. A person can tell what form his day will take and then work toward achieving it, thereby producing more.

2. **An effective time organization makes you a more organized person.** Putting items in their right place reduces the unnecessary time spent in search of missing files, stationery items, documents, folders, paperwork, and so on. To ensure better usage of time, people keep their workspace, booths, meeting area, conference room, or study area tidy

and well arranged. Also, time management helps individuals learn how to use things properly.

3. **Proven time organization makes you more confident, as it lifts your morale.** Due to time organization, you will be able to complete a given assignment within the time allocated for it. This benefit will cause you to be well admired in your place of work and among your colleagues.

Individuals who know the importance of time are the ones who manage to single themselves out from the crowd. People who complete work at the right time are well-liked by other people and are always the point of attraction in all places.

4. **People who stick to a time plan are the ones who understand their goals and objectives within the shortest possible period.** Making optimal use of time helps workers to meet

up with goals far before the time limit and complete a task when it is necessary.

5. **Active time organization helps you reach the peak of success quickly and remain fixed at the zenith for a more extended period.** If your reason for working is merely for the sake of it, you will fail to make an impression and will be less likely to be reckoned within your organization. Effective time organization plays a critical role in promoting a person's output. Productivity increases significantly when individuals manage their time correctly.

6. **Improved time organization helps in better planning and, ultimately, better forecasting.** People learn to organize things better and can predict where they will be in the next five years.

7. **People who complete a given task promptly are less prone to stress and anxiety.** Bear in mind that there is no sense in frittering away time only to be

stressed out later on. Complete all pending tasks at the right time, and then you will have plenty of free time for your family members and acquaintances.

8. **Time organization makes it possible for a person to prioritize tasks and activities at their workplace.** It is not wise to remain foolish enough to stay overloaded. Do not be too quick to say yes to all requests that come your way. Time organization makes it easier for a person to take on a deliberate approach in life.

How to Organize Your Time

- P**lan well**. Have a proper plan for your day before it even starts. Set up a to-do list or a task plan. Put into writing all vital tasks and activities that you need to complete in just one day with a specific amount of time assigned for each job. Assignments that take higher precedence should come at the top of the list, after which you should include those with less demanding importance. Finish following tasks one after the other; do not start a new job until after having completed older ones. Make sure also to mark the completed tasks and complete each assignment within the allotted time frame.

- **Set time limits**. Set time limits for yourself, and do everything possible to complete tasks before the stipulated time limits. Do not wait until your supervisors demand assignments from you all the time. Endeavor to take responsibility for your work. The only person in the best position to set time limits is you. Ponder on the time you will need to dedicate to each activity and the number of days it will take. You can keep track of important dates using a planner, comparing it against the stipulated time limits.

- **Allot responsibilities**. Do not agree with every single thing that is being asked of you at your organization. Learn not to be the one doing everything. There is always someone else available to take on the tasks. You should also never consent to functions that will prove difficult to complete. Assignments should be assigned to other employees based on interests and their areas of expertise to be completed within a given time frame. People who have limited knowledge about a thing tend to require extra time to complete a task compared to someone who knows the work well.

- **Adopt the use of a day-to-day planner**. You can use a paper or digital planner, depending on your preferences. The secret to it is keeping a record of all your tasks, duties, activities, and so on. Also, you need to have an accessible way to go back to them on a day-to-day basis. Use an organizer to allow your brain a break. It is difficult to recollect everything; hence, do not sweat it.

- **Set short and long-term goals**. Embarking on tasks and activities in a company without having definite goals and objectives can be likened to a captain who has lost his way at sea. Indeed, you would be off track. Carrying out regular goal-setting can give you a definite direction concerning what you need to do to achieve specific results. To attain essential and lasting goals, recognize smaller milestone goals as you go. For instance, if you have a target that needs to be reached within six months, you might require setting more modest goals to improve on some specific skills. Your goals should be precise, determinate, attainable, significant, and time-based.

- **Manage your schedule**. Putting time aside to finish vital assignments on your task list is essential in time organization. You may contemplate disregarding some specific time brackets on your schedule to be assured of enough time to attend to each assignment without having interruptions or other intruding conferences. You must also determine which appointments are worth visiting and those who are not. If you sense that you have little or nothing to contribute, you should not hesitate to decline such conferences. If you ever detect the need to do this, you must be civil and well-mannered about it. Be thoughtful enough to send a prior notice, most preferably, an email informing them of your absence that includes your reasons.

- **Organize tasks**. Prioritizing can be very tasking, but it gets better with time and practice. You can exercise your prioritization skills by drawing a to-do list. Tick off those activities that you need to do in a day, week, month, and so on. Putting down everything you need, whether on paper or an electronic device, will help you accomplish tasks based on their level of priority or ease of completion. If you require assistance, you might consider asking your colleague or boss (who is likely good at prioritizing tasks) how they get their work done.

Having knowledge of deadlines and how each assignment affects others and the targets set by the organization can help you complete specific tasks before the rest of your colleagues. Tasks should be completed based on their level of importance.

- **Dedicate your time and energy to things you are most passionate about**. A large number of individuals try to be everything to everyone. You are likely to know someone who fits that description - or perhaps, this may even be describing you. You could offer to take part in committees at your place of work, volunteer at social gatherings, or agree to teach kids how to play basketball despite knowing that you have little time at your disposal. At one point or the other, we find ourselves in this situation. The result of such is that we become beat up, exhausted, and hateful. Devote yourself to completing a task or two at most, and decline any other offer in a civil manner.

- **Check for potential problems**. All of us waste hours going to closed stores or art centers or have missed a train due to invalid information. Your plans can even be disrupted by simple road construction. Ensure to keep your monthly itinerary up-to-date, and try to add in alternatives for specific tasks if you can see a setback coming. Check the local newspapers for reports, and always browse the internet for opening hours and train schedules.

- **Sleep at least seven hours every night**. A lack of good sleep can result in several psychological and physical problems. You must understand that it is never just about getting more done, but instead, it is about performing better.

- **Morning day routine**. The morning is a vital part of the day. A wholesome and fruitful morning will create an atmosphere for a productive day overall; hence, ensure to take morning routines seriously. Begin making plans for your morning the night before. Pick out the clothes you will wear the next day and set targets. Get up the moment your alarm goes off; do not snooze the alarm. Drink some water and practice exercises to get you revitalized. Follow your schedule strictly all through the morning, and minimize diversions to start your day off productively.

- **Select your clothes for the next day.** You do not want to spend time in the morning, deliberating on what to wear. The night before, choose an outfit for the coming day. Spread it out on a table, or hang it up in your closet. When the morning arrives, you'll be able to throw on your clothes and welcome the day quickly.

- **Set targets for the next day.** It is recommended for you to have three to four small goals daily to increase your output. Before you go to bed each night, draw a list of things you wish to accomplish the following day. By doing so, you can determine what you require from each morning and focus your attention accordingly.

- **Do not hit the snooze button**. While the few additional minutes of sleep sound tempting when you are sleepy, hitting the snooze button is never the best way to start your morning. Doing so may even make you more fatigued because you are continually disturbing your sleep pattern. When your alarm awakens you during deep and relaxing sleep, but you hit the snooze button, you revert to a lighter sleeping state. This type of sleep will not provide additional rest, and instead, it can make you more exhausted in the long run. Rather than snoozing the alarm, set the alarm to the exact time you need to get up. Do not place the alarm for 8:30 so you can have the pleasure of turning off the alarm and then getting up at 8:45. On the contrary, set the alarm for 8:45, and get up without hitting snooze.

- **Rise at least two hours early**. You want to make sure you wake up with time to spare for showering, getting dressed, eating breakfast, and doing any other important things you need to do before work or school. Make it a goal to get up about two hours before you need to be somewhere. For instance, assuming you must be at your place of work by 8:00 in the morning, get up at 6:00. This setup is subject to things like your commute; you may need to get up earlier. If it takes you an hour to commute to work, for example, you'll have to set out by 7:00 in the morning, and you will then want to aim at awaking at 5:00.

- **Eat a healthy breakfast**. You should never go without breakfast. Doing so will only leave you fatigued and sleepy all through the day. For your breakfast, avoid heavily processed foods and those with high sugar content. Consume a healthy breakfast that includes whole grains, proteins, and fruits. Opt for things like fruit and yogurt, oatmeal, and a green smoothie. Avoid pastries such as doughnuts or microwaveable breakfast foods.

- **Begin your day with exercise**. It is not until you have visited the gym that you can boost your energy. A little amount of exercise can go a long way in helping you begin the day with a lot of strength and vigor while reducing your stress levels to the bare minimum. Even a ten-minute exercise can turn the course of your day around for the better, keeping you energized all day long. You can go for a short walk around the neighborhood, practice some yoga exercises in the privacy of your room, or do a ten-minute walk on your treadmill.

- **Stay off the internet first thing in the morning**. Until you have completed everything you need to do, stay away from your phone and laptop. Set strict rules for yourself regarding when you can be on the internet. For instance, you can decide not to look at your phone until you have finished a minimum of three tasks. Social media can have very distracting effects on people. Make efforts to log out of social media platforms like Twitter and Instagram the night before. In addition to this, stay away from things like news websites. You want to avoid starting off the day with a disheartening report.

- **Plan your time carefully**. While going about your daily routine, it is crucial to keep track of time, as it is very easy to get carried away while taking a shower or eating your breakfast. To prevent this, you need to allow time for each activity and ensure that you stick to each period of time. First, though, you should make a list of all the activities you usually engage in daily and how much time you need to complete all these tasks. For instance, you may have 15 minutes to take a shower, get dressed, arrange your hair, and eat your breakfast. All you need to do is divide these activities and assign a specific amount of time to each one. While doing this, don't take your eyes off the clock to prevent yourself from spending too much time on one activity.

- **Do not multitask**. You should make it a practice to take things one step at a time as you proceed with your activities for the day. Many people think they will save more time by multitasking. However, the truth is that you will end up wasting more time and would likely be less productive at the end of the day. To be productive, complete one task at a time. That way, you will be able to channel your energy to the task at hand and complete it rather than starting multiple tasks at once and stopping midway. In addition, keep your mind off the next task on your to-do list. Although it may be challenging to keep your mind from wandering, make a concerted effort to direct your attention back to the present task.

Your Quick Start Action Step:

1. Think about the top ten activities that you waste time on in your life.

2. Write down the five most important activities of those ten imagined, and rank them from most to least severe.

3. Write down the reasons you think you waste time on them; include two reasons for each of the five.

4. Now write five ways in which organizing your time will benefit you.

Chapter 4: Organizing Family Activities

Chapter 4: Organizing Family Activities

Your daily routine could be so fixed that you hardly have time to have fun with the kids. For instance, you could be busy with work, cleaning the home, going to school, and sleeping. In order to have spare time, you will need to avoid wasting time on unnecessary activities. Also, you can look for ways to make your daily chores more interesting by turning them into games so you could include your children in your daily tasks.

Taking a closer look at your schedule, you will discover that you might still be able to find free time in your busy schedule. It is always good to spend some quality time with family. By being organized, you will be able to make some free time and reduce stress.

Why It's Important to Organize Your Family Activities

To strengthen the family bond. The primary reason for making out time for family is to ensure that you develop stronger ties with them. In most cases, kids tend to join bad groups because they feel welcomed by members of such groups, and they view them as family.

Your children need to be reassured that they are part of the family, and as such, they need to feel a sense of belonging and security. By spending quality time with them, you're indirectly telling them to always turn to you and look up to you for anything. Therefore, spending quality time with family will ensure that a deep, warm, and strong family bond is established.

To make time to talk and listen. Communication is essential to have a healthy family relationship. Spending time with your family will allow you to speak and listen to each other, thereby resolving any differences within the family.

Today, most parents often assume that taking the time to talk with their kids will be difficult, if not a waste of time, compared with talking to adults. However, parents often forget about their early days and how it felt when they were about the same age as their kids. Generally, children are often attracted to those who spend time listening to whatever they need to say. You likely may have felt the same way when you were their age.

Also, keep in mind that listening involves more than just hearing the words your child is saying while making sure you feel the message your child is trying to express. Even if it doesn't make much sense to you, it certainly does to them.

While listening to them is essential, it is also necessary to avoid jumping to conclusions, cutting them off mid-way, criticizing their ideas, or enforcing your viewpoints upon them. To show them that you're genuinely involved in the conversation, you need to suspend whatever you're doing and give them your undivided attention. Discuss a relevant subject such as sex, alcohol, or drugs directly with your kids - most notably, the teenagers. Most importantly, ensure you set a good example yourself.

To teach your children valuable lessons in life. If you fail to teach your children at home, they will be explained elsewhere. As parents, it would be disheartening if your children were to learn life's valuable lessons the hard way, such as by experiencing the pain that results from making a wrong choice.

Indeed, you can't teach your children everything, and they will learn a few lessons from their personal experiences in life. However, parents must spend time with their family to discuss some pertinent issues. Such time allows the family to put forth points or challenging conditions they are faced with and then discuss such issues as a family.

During these discussions, parents should try to seek the opinions of their children and discuss with them the matter at hand. This way, they will learn and understand how to handle various situations in life in more efficient ways.

To show affection, appreciation, and encouragement. Spending family time together allows every member of the family to show love to each other. Such displays of affection can include giving a warm hug, holding hands to pray, kind and thoughtful words of encouragement, and the giving of gifts. According to researchers, teenagers who were showed affection by being hugged, commended for a good deed, or kissed are more likely to perform better at school than those who lacked such experiences.

One good way to show affection is by asking each member of the family how they spent their day and what activities they engaged in during the day. It is often easier to criticize than to give commendations; therefore, make a conscious effort to focus on the positive qualities of each person, and tell your kids what you notice and appreciate about them. By doing so, you will be indirectly teaching them good values.

To instill family values in your children. Nowadays, it is vital to instill family values in your children to avoid being misled by the growing number of divorce cases.

As a parent, you need to set good examples for your children, because they tend to imitate your behavior and the attitude you show toward them. If you are always away from home, for instance, your children are more likely to follow that example in the future.

Thus, by spending time with your family, you will be instilling positive family values in them and building in them a sense of self-worth.

To inculcate family rituals and traditions. The little things or daily routines you perform daily or on special occasions will help create a sense of satisfaction, a sense of belonging, and inner peace within the family. Daily rituals, such as the way you greet each other, how you say goodbye on your way out, or what you say or do at mealtimes and bedtimes, can all go a long way to make the family time you spend worthwhile.

Most families that come together to celebrate special events such as wedding anniversaries, birthdays, or holidays often benefit from these gatherings, because they learn from such traditions and what happens on these occasions.

To accept the differences in each person. Family time allows each member of the family to appreciate, commend, and cherish the uniqueness in each other. By spending quality time together, you will get to know that everyone is unique in their own way. During such occasions, ensure that each family member feels excited and that everyone is shown the respect they deserve.

Avoid the mistake of forcing other members of the family to be like you or pressuring them into hiding their feelings or differences. Instead, make them feel proud of who they are.

To keep in touch with friends and relatives. The kind of society we live in today does not encourage spending time with family and interacting with friends. However, during a crisis, we can be assured that we can always turn to our family. Our children can also feel secure and happy, knowing that they have someone to turn to. Moreover, such experiences will help your children make good friends later in life.

To share the chores. During family time, you can seize the opportunity to teach your children how to be responsible by giving them specific duties or tasks while you supervise them.

However, do not be too hard on them, but rather try to show a sense of humor, and remember to give commendation for a job well done.

If you spend more time with your family, gradually a special kind of relationship based on intimacy and trust will develop. This approach is necessary if you wish to have a healthy family relationship. This trust level usually becomes relevant when children are allowed to make meaningful contributions during a decision-making process.

To help you connect better with your children. The busy world out there makes most parents overlook the critical role of parenting and the part it plays in the educational life of their children. Most parents don't realize that family time offers parents the opportunity to get involved in their children's learning process.

Parents and other family members need to make time to spend together. According to research, when parents get themselves involved in the family, their children are more likely to:

- Get high test scores and grades
- Leave high school with an excellent graduating grade
- Proceed to college and attain higher education
- Develop positive attitudes and be well-behaved

Family time could involve simple activities, such as reading a story to your kids at bedtime, going through their homework with them, attending a PTA meeting, discussing your child's progress with their teachers, or any other activities that are related to their academic life. It could also involve asking your child how their day was at school, which helps if done every day.

How to Plan for Family Activities

1. **Ensure your mornings work out well for you.** On most mornings, we are often disorganized and tend to make mistakes during the rush. However, since if you take things easy, you can arrive at

your child's school calm and still have enough energy to face the day.

2. **Have a menu plan.** If you don't have one already, it's advised that you start a menu plan today. Having a good menu plan help take away the daily worry of deciding what to cook for breakfast, and it will also help you stick to your budget. It is often suggested to start with a menu plan for dinners, and once you get a handle on the process, you can then begin to add breakfasts and lunches.

3. **Create a family launch pad or command center.** Try to have a central location where all the daily items that are needed by your family can be kept. By doing so, it will be much easier to find and use anything that is required.

4. **Design a weekly visual schedule.** Developing an accessible visual schedule or a calendar for each week's activities and placing them where all the members of the family can see it is an excellent way

to encourage everyone to be more organized. This process will also help your kids grow into independent adults.

5. **Plan for success.** Reflect on the challenging tasks in your daily routine, and try to find ways of simplifying such tasks. For instance, you should think about the following things:

- Selecting your child's school uniforms first thing in the morning or the night before.

- Having a box for hair accessories where everything needed is kept together, such as a hairbrush, hair spray, and hair ties.

- Keeping a homework box where everything you need for your child's homework is stored for easy access.

- Keeping your daughter's dance bags in the last drawer of your central launchpad so that everything she needs is held together and ready for dance class afternoons.

6. **Design a cleaning routine.** Everyone must decide when to clean, how to clean, and how often to clean the house. The most important thing is having a routine that works well for you and sticking to it. When you find a routine, and you consistently stay on track, it can help you minimize the stress of cleaning chores.

7. **Get your children involved in cleaning and household chores.** Parents often feel that involving their children in cooking, cleaning, washing, and other household chores is an extra chore on its own. After all, it will take a longer time to teach them, yet the results are not guaranteed. In the end, it would be as good as doing it yourself but with extra stress. However, such activities will help teach your child essential life skills and give them a higher sense of self-worth, fulfillment, and independence.

8. **Create a chore chart.** Utilizing a regular schedule of chores for your children will help them develop a sense of responsibility. There are various ways to monitor these chores and add an incentive or compensation to each completed task, such as pocket money.

9. **Have a personal to-do list.** By nature, I'm a very religious list-maker, but I have this bad habit of scribbling on any paper scrap, which eventually gets misplaced. But now, I'm making a more conscious effort to have an organized to-do list that will help sort out tasks according to category. It will also keep everything together in one place. Besides, it helps me to prioritize all my tasks.

To make your weekly to-do list more easily accessible, you can print it out such that you can always sort out family-related and work-related tasks while on the move.

10. **Prioritize the most important things to your family.** What matters in one family differs from others. Therefore, each family must determine what matters the most to them. Then prioritize those organizational tools that are likely to be most useful in the home. How you want your children to view your home after they grow up and live on their own is a good starting point for you to review your priorities.

11. **Identify time wasters.** By detecting and eliminating time-wasting activities, you can create extra time for you and your family. To identify such events, you may need to sit down and discuss the issue as a team.

12. **Prepare for family outings.** Ensure that you make plans for pleasurable family outings and ones that every member of the family will enjoy. These plans can be done by choosing activities that everyone, including your children,

can participate in and be excited about. If you observe that your teenage child doesn't seem to be excited about group outings, you can rekindle his or her interest by allowing him or her to choose the activities for the outing.

13. **Make good use of Saturdays.** If your work permits to rest on Saturdays, you can make good use of that day for family-related activities. You could spend the day riding bicycles with the kids or eating ice cream. Another suggestion is to go on a day visit to a nearby tourist attraction center. Such outings will help your children get out of the house, and they will also learn more about their community. Other Saturday activities could include:

- Spending some time outdoors at the closest national park or beach

- A visit to a fire station to learn what it takes to be a fireman

- Visiting a science or an art museum
- Participating in volunteer work together with your kids

14. **Find a family hobby.** Finding something interesting that everyone will like doing is a great way to spend some quality time together weekly. For instance, you can spend time with your kids while teaching them a new skill. Such activities include:

    - Teaching your children how to build a simple game (if your son or daughter loves playing video games)
    - Teaching them how to cook (if your son or daughter loves cooking)
    - Joining a robotics club together (if they like playing with electronics)

Your Quick Start Action Step:

1. Ask your partner if he or she is happy with the amount of time you spend with them daily. If your partner isn't around,

ask any of your children around you at the time.
2. Ask them how and where they want you to improve concerning family time.
3. Now, write down the specific family activities you want to engage them in for the next month.

Chapter 5: Achieving a Clutter-Free Home

Chapter 5: Achieving a Clutter-Free Home

Many people love the idea of living a simple, uncluttered life; a life with less stress, less to organize, less debt, less to clean, and more money and energy to pursue their passions. They have considered getting rid of unnecessary possessions and are ready to declutter. However, many people don't know where they should start.

After so much brainstorming, many still feel anxious and confused when it comes to decluttering their homes. But the good news is that the process of decluttering shouldn't be as painful as some make it appear. Various experiences demonstrate that decluttering can be a lot of fun.

However, as fun as it can be, decluttering can also be challenging. Whether you decide to declutter by using downsizing efforts or by simplifying your life, both require effort and sacrifice. It is often suggested that you tackle the entire process in stages. For example, you can start by taking on a room, space, or a small zone within a place such as your laundry cabinets. Once you've completed the present task, you can then move on to the next room or space. The success you experience from such smaller tasks will boost your confidence, and you will be ready for more significant jobs.

Note that a decluttered home = a decluttered life; therefore, ensure that you solve every clutter need.

You might find it surprising to know that you don't need sophisticated tools to declutter your home. Sometimes all you need is three baskets or bins tagged for five different purposes. These include the following:

- **The put-away bin:** These are items that are found where they aren't supposed to be that need to be returned to their designated spots. Examples are a teacup in the bathroom or a pair of socks in the kitchen.

- **The recycle bin:** This bin contains items that could be recycled, such as plastic bags, glass, and paper.

- **Mend/fix bin:** This bin includes items that need to be cleaned or repaired, such as your favorite pair of shoes.

- **Trash bin:** Items that are irredeemable are kept in this designated bin and can be emptied into the family trash immediately for disposal.

- **Donate bin:** This bin is meant for items that you no longer need, but that can be useful to others, such as a charitable organization or other individuals.

If these bins are not available, you can make use of cardboard boxes as well. The containers can be kept in a central location in your home; you can keep them in each room as you declutter. One important thing to avoid is searching for containers in the middle of a decluttering process; it's best to set up the bins before you commence.

Why a Clutter-Free Home Is Important

There are a couple of benefits you will derive from taking time to declutter your home. Some of these benefits are highlighted below:

- **Financial:** We could be coerced into buying duplicates of items we already own if we are not cautious. Clutter costs lots of money, especially when we can't find things that we know we possess.

- **Time:** Owning so many possessions consumes more time than we could ever imagine. When every item is in its right place, we can save nearly an hour per day. You could then use this amount of time for yourself and your family.

- **Space:** Decluttering your home means that you will have more space for playing, living, and working. Clutter-free spaces are more attractive and can be used for greater purposes.

- **Emotional:** When we declutter our life, we can live a more balanced, peaceful, and energy-filled life. Such a healthy way of living will improve our health, make us happy, and reduce anxiety.

- **Find stuff:** When we declutter our home, it will help reduce the time that would have wasted searching for stuff.

How to Declutter Your Home

Bathrooms. You can start with your medicine cabinet in the bathroom. Firstly, bring everything out and dispose of expired medications, lotions, and other skincare products. Whatever you still wish to keep should be returned to the cabinet without delays. Keep the items you regularly use at eye level.

You can then proceed to any other cabinet drawers. As done before, take everything out of the drawer, and carry out a fast evaluation of what item(s) you wish to keep and those that need to be disposed of. Once you're done sorting that out, return the items you want to keep into the drawers, with the things most important stored in the first drawers.

At this point, repeat the same exercise with your tub/shower. Lastly, remove whatever item you find below your bathroom sink and declutter such items.

Every stray item would eventually be sorted out into any of the five baskets/bins you've already labeled according to their purpose.

Bedrooms. The first thing you need to do is make your bed. If the bed is unmade, it will be difficult to notice any progress while decluttering a room.

You can then proceed to remove all the clothes on the nightstands, along with any other item that doesn't belong there, and put them in one of the tagged bins. Other items include an already completed book, a broken eyeglass, or a dried-up pen.

You should also do the same with the tops of your chests and dressers. Take your time searching for any clothing that is hanging randomly after putting each item in its place. Any cloth that needs to be folded or hung should go into the put-away bin.

Make sure to go through each drawer carefully. Pull everything out, search for clothes that you no longer wear, and transfer them into the donation bin. Fold the rest and arrange them back into the drawer.

If you have a vanity table or a desk in your bedroom, this should be the next thing you tackle. Avoid the temptation to shove items back into drawers, and instead, place them in your put-away bin or recycle bin, especially items you haven't used for the past six months. Fold or hang and store any clothing you still need, and keep them in their proper places.

Closet and clothing. The best way to declutter your closet is to declutter all your clothing by type first. This technique means that you start with your dresses, then denim, shoes, and boots.

This method makes it easier to decide what items to keep and which things need to be tossed away. For instance, if you focus on your denim collection at once, you will see that deciding which pair of jeans to keep or discard will be easier. This approach also saves time compared with trying to sort out all the clothes in your closet at once.

After sorting out all the type of clothing, you're likely to have four piles to tackle:

1. Discard any item that was randomly abandoned at the wrong spot. For example, if you found a tie in your closet, you can put it back in your dresser.

2. All dirty laundry should be kept in the hamper or transferred to the laundry room.

3. All worn-out clothes that need cleaning or mending should be packed and sent to the dry cleaner or tailor accordingly.

4. All items that you have no use for should go into the donation bin and dropped off

at a consignment store or donation center.

Entryways, foyers, and mudrooms. Although you may not have a mudroom or foyer in your home, you most certainly have an entryway that leads into the house. Regardless of the size, you need to declutter it regularly to make the entryway functional.

If there is any console, tables, or desk in your entryway, this might be the best place to start from. Just as you did for your closet, go through each drawer, and empty all the contents in it. Now, decide which items need to be tossed or kept. As much as you can, decongest the top drawer to make enough space for your keys and other essential items.

Kitchen. Due to the many different activities that take place in the kitchen, keeping it clutter-free can be challenging. Because of activities such as- cooking, eating, and socializing, various types of items are held in the kitchen. In this instance, as well, you should focus on one group of items at a time. For example, you may decide to declutter the glassware, bakeware, or cutting boards.

You may begin by completely emptying the top cabinet, selecting items that are still needed, and tossing those you no longer need. You can then return the useful items to their proper places. Next, focus on the lower cabinets and the space below your kitchen sink.

The countertops should not be left out. Decongest the countertops as much as possible by moving items that litter the countertops, and keep them in the appropriate storage spaces. Only items that you use daily should be kept on the countertops.

The last thing you need to do is to return anything that doesn't belong in the kitchen back to their rightful storage spaces.

Living room. Aside from the kitchen, the living room is yet another problematic place to declutter. The reason is because of the vital functions of this room. Usually, the living room doesn't have ample storage spaces. It is often suggested that:

- Items that are used regularly have permanent storage space. Such items include magazines, books, and remote controls.

- You also declutter this space regularly.

You can begin with the console, side tables, and bookcases. Next, you can focus on your coffee table and entertainment area. Just as in previous cases, empty all the items in the store and decide what object needs to be returned to its proper storage spaces and those that need to be tossed.

Now, you can shift your focus to electronics. Any gadgets not directly connected to your home theater system or television should be removed. Then ask yourself if you still use it or if it still works. Items such as gaming equipment, chargers, and other gadgets should be kept in their designated places.

Finally, focus on the toys. Examine each toy to sort out those that are damaged. Again, ask yourself if it's still functional and whether your kid still plays with it. Finding an answer to these questions will determine whether you should store or recycle each toy.

Your Quick Start Action Step:

1. Make a mental picture of the level of disorganization in every room in your house, including your bathroom and kitchen.

2. Envision how you want those rooms to look after organizing them.

3. Now, write down the rooms you want to declutter, from the easiest to the most difficult, and how long it will take you to finish each one.

4. To learn more about decluttering your home, check out the book from the author entitled "Declutter your Home: Simple Step-by-Step Decluttering Strategies on How to Declutter and Organize to De-Stress and Simplify your Life" in the online store.

Chapter 6: Organizing Your Finances

Chapter 6: Organizing Your Finances

Decluttering your home will make it look cozy and neat. The interesting thing to note is that all it takes is the simple process of deciding what items are no longer necessary and should be discarded immediately. Discarding certain items may be a tough choice to make; however, we usually know what items we still need and those we don't.

This situation is not the case when it comes to decluttering your financial life, though. The entire process involved is difficult to understand and even more challenging to apply. What makes physical decluttering comparatively easier is that items you no longer need are easier to notice, like the unused dumbbell in your bedroom that hits your toe at least twice a day. With physical objects, you'll often be reminded that they need to be tossed. On the contrary, cluttered money is not as visible.

It might interest you to know that the same principles that will help a newbie declutter his or her financial life are also applicable to minimalists.

In the financial world, messy finances usually lead to worry and anxiety. One of the best decisions you can ever make is to decide to simplify your economic life. To oversee your spending, you may need to cut down on your bills, expense, and purchases.

Why It Is Necessary to Organize Your Finances

Organizing your finances will help you see clearly how to allocate your money the best and then provide ideas on what items to purchase based on your financial status. It will protect you against the pain that comes with overspending and being in so much debt. Many feel that budgeting prevents them from enjoying their lives; however, what it does is ensures that you enjoy stuff within your financial limitations.

Although it requires a lot of calculations and brainstorming, it will pay off in the end. Additionally, it comes with a lot of life-enhancing benefits, such as those highlighted below:

- **You gain control over your money**: You will be cautious about how you save and spend your money, and it will help you avoid the stress of suddenly adjusting to a lack of funds because you failed to plan how to spend your money initially. Budgeting also offers you the opportunity to decide whether you want to sacrifice long-term benefits for short-term spending.

- **Help you focus on your money goals:** Unnecessary spending can be avoided if you properly plan how you should spend your money. Any item or service that will not help you achieve your financial goals can easily be avoided.

- **It makes you conscious of what is going on with your money:** You know exactly how much you're expecting, how soon it will be spent, and what you will spend it on. Being financially organized will save you from wondering where your money went at the end of every month. Also, you will be able to figure out how much you're worth financially and what you can afford to buy, save, and invest. You will also be able to cut down on your debts.

- **Helps you organize your spending and savings better:** When you consciously divide your money into different categories of savings and expenditures, you will be able to monitor your spending and know exactly how much spending is required on each. With that, it will be much easier to adjust when necessary. Such an organization can also be used for reference purposes in filing your financial statements, receipts, and bills. In addition, your financial transactions can be presented at tax time or for creditor questions and will help you save some energy and time as well.

- **You will be able to save for expected and unexpected costs:** By being organized, you will be able to plan and set some money aside for unforeseen expenses.

- **Helps you to discuss financial matters with your family:** Automation can assist you in quickly considering how money is being spent with them especially if the funds will be significantly shared with your partner or other members of the family. This method will foster teamwork, help you pursue common financial goals, and help to avoid financial conflicts revolving around how money was spent.

- **Helps you to produce extra money:** It will make it easier for you to avoid unnecessary spending, penalties for late fees, and incurred interests.

How to Plan Your Finances

Step 1: Define specific financial goals (with actual figures). Many people often suggest that you can begin decluttering your finances by clearing all outstanding bills and financial obligations first to determine your financial standing. Although this is a crucial step, it shouldn't be your starting point.

First, you need to be clear about your financial goals, or it will be difficult for you to organize your finances logically.

Your financial goal shouldn't be an arbitrary one, such as saving up to four months' worth of living expenses in an emergency account. That translates to nothing meaningful if there is no actual figure to relate with.

It is, however, more meaningful if you put it this way: "I want to save $7,000 in an emergency account by the end of 2019." This statement is much better than saying the following: "I want to open an emergency account."

Once you're done with the numbers, you can then proceed to the next step by developing habits and financial behaviors that will assist you in achieving your goal.

Step 2: Know where you stand. The next step is to determine your financial standing. At this point, you may need to gather all your financial documents such as your credit card statements, bank statements, loan papers, bills, mortgage papers, and insurance documents. All of these will help you get a clear picture of your financial worth, how much money you are expecting, and how much you plan to spend monthly.

You may be wondering why such an evaluation is necessary. Author Kate Northrup, in her bestselling book "Money: A Love Story", said that most people couldn't account for how much they earned and how much they've spent within the $100 range, all within the previous month.

It can be difficult, if not impossible, to declutter if you can't properly account for your financial status. Most individuals, especially those in debt, try as much as possible to avoid going through this part, as they fear numbers. However, if you really want to get your financial situation together, you must decide where you want to be (Step 1), but you can't get to where you want to be without knowing where you presently stand financially.

Below are some suggestions for what to watch out for, while going through your financial documents:

- How much money do you earn as a monthly salary?

- How much extra money do you earn each month from investments or side hustles?

- How much money do you owe?

- What kinds of debts do you have? What are the interest rates? How much do you pay back monthly?

- How much money are you saving for retirement, and is it enough?

- How much do you have in your emergency savings account?

Only a few areas have been discussed above for you to think about before you continue with your investigation. However, you can also look for other loopholes to investigate.

Some miscellaneous non-monthly expenses usually catch people off guard. These include costs such as medical bills, money spent on Christmas shopping, dental fees, annual fees, and web hosting expenses.

Step 3: Figure out where you're leaking money. If the whole process of decluttering your finances is new to you, then you may lose money. This money can be lost in different ways, such as:

- Buying unnecessary products or services
- Buying at very high prices
- Payment of fees or bills

At this point, you must look at how you spend and take specific steps to regulate your spending where necessary. When you reduce the amount of money you waste, you will be able to manage your financial affairs without difficulties.

Here is where beginners can begin looking for leaks:

- Do you purchase additional products or services? In other words, do you buy things you do not need? These products or services could include cable subscriptions, movie tickets, and a lot more. Do you purchase products at very high rates?

- Are there possibilities for reducing your bills? For example, you can search for a cheaper insurance premium.

Here is where you can look after having the basics covered:

- Is there any way you can reduce the fees on some of your accounts if not all? You can search for an online bank that operates without fees or tries bargaining for a lower annual percentage rate (APR).

Since the goal is not only to save money, people are advised to use different ways to make extra cash. These include things such as selling old properties or by starting up a side business outside of their regular jobs.

Step 4: After figuring out where your money is leaking from, the next thing to do is to go paperless. This method means transferring all your financial files to a cloud system. This approach will help you access all your financial details without the difficulties that come with bulky paper files. You can easily search for whichever file you need on the cloud system.

The paper files are scanned, well arranged, and then uploaded to a safe cloud system. New financial details should be uploaded at least once a month. The only part of this step that takes a lot of time is when you have to scan all the paper files you've had for years and manually transfer them to a cloud system. After this step is completed, you can relax and stop worrying about a stack of paper files.

Another advantage of transferring all your paper files to a cloud networking service is that you can keep a record for everything going on in your financial life with the help of tools like Mint.com and other similar services. Mint.com can be used to set up budgets and goals and review fees and investments.

Step 5: Automate as much as you can. In a bid to be in control of your budget, you may need to automate it as much as you can. Carl Richard, the author of "The One-page Financial Plan", explains in his book that those who have thoughts of saving may end up not saving at all.

In decluttering your finances, below are a couple of the areas where you can automate your money:

- **Savings**: In decluttering your finances, you must automate your savings. You can set up an automatic saving plan in which money is transferred to your savings account from your checking account. For instance, a certain amount, such as $500, is transferred to a particular account for emergency purposes at least once every month.

- **Retirement and investments**: You can go to the HR department at work to set up the automatic deposit of your paycheck. The process of doing this is straightforward, and apart from losing extra cash, you have absolutely nothing to lose. Also, if you have an IRA (individual retirement account), you can create an automatic deposit into an account of your choice.

Step 6: Avoid being in debt. This step can seem challenging to do, but it is achievable. There is great satisfaction in paying in full for what you buy without having to be indebted to anyone.

So, how do you get rid of your debt? First, save up to $1,000 to fund your emergencies. After doing this, make a list of all the money you owe, and then start paying off the debt one after the other, from the lowest amount to the highest.

Once the lowest debt is cleared, add the amount you paid to the next smallest debt to keep the ball rolling until all your debts are removed. This process is known as the debt snowball.

Step 7: Do you need help with your financial life? Don't be too shy or proud to get one. Put yourself in order before inviting a helper.

You could hire a personal financial accountant, or you could opt for counseling, especially in areas you are having problems with. You don't have to do both at once, but make sure you get help whenever you need one.

A financial accountant could help you with your taxes, while counseling could help solve financial problems like debt, overspending, and a lot more.

Your Quick Start Action Step:

1. Make a mental note of your needs and your wants.

2. Go through your bank statements, and highlight irrelevant things you have spent money on.

3. Now, write down your budget for the next month and your financial goals (or target) for the next three months.

To learn more about financial success and solving debt problems, check out "Minimalist Budget: Simple and Practical Budgeting Strategies to Save Money, Avoid Compulsive Spending, Pay Off Debt and Simplify Your Life" by Marie S. Davenport in the online store.

Chapter 7: Decluttering with Others in Your Life

Chapter 7: Decluttering with Others in Your Life

Some of us have been in a relationship with someone who we thought was the one, and we've experienced one thing: inconsistency. During the first few months of a relationship, your partner seems perfect, does everything right, and treats you well - then, they stop.

In times like this, decluttering your relationship is what you should do. Decluttering with others is a process that means avoiding people who become toxic to your life and affect your happiness. Your emotional and mental health should be your highest priority; therefore, learn to let go of people who impact your health negatively.

Leaving a relationship can be painful, no matter how toxic or offensive it is. We find it very difficult to let go of friends, family members, spouses, and business partners who don't value us or limit us. The reason is because of the effort, time, and resources we've put into building such relationships. Often, the ones who are so dear to us and who we have known for many years cause the most considerable pain.

The pain can reach a point where you would choose to make the hard decision of getting rid of them instead of sticking around and enduring the pain. However, in some cases, the drowning thoughts, worry, and depression are due to the individual's inability to manage relationships. You are in control of your feelings, and how you choose to respond to any situation is a matter of choice. The moment you understand this theory is the moment you will be able to live a quiet life that is free of aches.

This chapter will talk about specific issues you may likely encounter in your relationship with people. It will also help to build up and improve your communication skills. It will also talk about unhealthy relationships and how to handle them.

Why It's Important to Declutter with Others in Your Life

1. You waste a lot of energy dealing with toxic people: You must stop remaining in unhealthy relationships. Stop talking to toxic people; you don't owe anyone an explanation for making such a decision except those you were close to. You can open up to them; it is not uncommon for friends or even family members to drift apart. It is your responsibility to protect your happiness and live a peaceful life. Therefore, no matter how long you've been friends with a person, once you realize that the relationship is toxic, cut them off. Being with toxic people is a massive waste of time and energy.

2. You'll have more time for yourself: Having quality time with yourself is very refreshing. When you declutter your relationship with others, it gives you time to have a better relationship with yourself. If you want to lead a more purposeful life, then allow more time to relate with yourself. There are many ways you can do to fill up the empty space you feel inside. You could revive the inner you, forgive yourself, and learn to love yourself, but the best way is by creating more time for yourself alone to reflect on things. Having toxic people around could hinder your alone time and further drown you with problems.

3. Being criticized continuously is exhausting: Constant criticism is not healthy as it negatively affects your mentality and results. Being criticized continually can make you doubt your worth. You may begin to lose control of yourself, always looking for others' approval and living below your standards, and adopting another's. Keeping people who judge you still is bad for you, therefore cut them off. You don't have to live your life based on someone else's judgment. Stay away from friends, family members, and other people who do not know your true worth and do not love and accept you for who you are.

4. You'll reach your goals sooner: Toxic people around you can delay you from reaching your goals. They take attention away from your goals. Once you begin to stay away from them, you'll get back on course.

5. You'll dedicate more time to the people that matter. Not all your friends are toxic;

there are most likely some who are genuine, and you should keep them. You can do this by spending more time with these people. Having new friends and talking with them can be very interesting, but they shouldn't take up all your time and effort. Disconnecting from those who don't add value to your life gives you enough time to strengthen your relationships with real friends. Aside from that, you also get to spend time with yourself.

How to Declutter with Others

You need to learn to love and hold yourself at very high esteem. With this, you won't condone any destructive relationship for any reason. The following are things you need to know about decluttering relationships:

- **Stop judging people around you:** You cannot get rid of people who do not care about you or respect you when you are doing the same thing to others. Stop judging people, and instead, care for them and value them for who they are. You are not in a position to change anybody, and so you shouldn't even attempt to do so. Accept people for who they are and not for who you want them to be. Lower your expectations of people if they are too high; we are all looking for someone who will love and value us for who we are. So, why set an unrealistic standard that no one can meet? Think deep before you cut anyone off; you could lose a diamond in search of glitter.

- **Stay away from people who make you unhappy:** Emotions or feelings can be contagious. Remain around happy people, and you will tend to become happy, but stay around unhappy people, and the reverse is the case. Some people are fond of complaining about everything, and they never seem to be satisfied with life. When you are always around such people, their misery can be transferred to you. Others tend to make you sad with their judgments and complain about your life - some of them do this without even knowing. The best thing you can do for yourself is to avoid them and have peace of mind.

- **Reduce your relationship with family members who affect you emotionally.** When it comes to family members, you cannot get rid of them, for they are a part of your existence. However, you can reduce your relationship with them. Set a boundary between you and that family member you love so much and can't completely cut off. This family member could be your favorite sibling, your best uncle or aunt, or even a parent who keeps nagging about your life, makes you feel unworthy of love and keeps opening up old wounds and makes life miserable. Since it is your responsibility to guard your heart, then there is no crime in avoiding those who keep hurting you. They are your family members, and yes, you love them, and you know they love you too and want the best for you, but this should not be done at the expense of your happiness.

- **Surround yourself with happy people:** The primary aim of decluttering your relationships with others is to have peace of mind and happiness. Therefore, happiness is a commodity sought after by all, including you. If you are looking for happiness, find happy people. Happy people always give you a reason to smile; they are always full of life, and you should surround yourself with them.

- **Surround yourself with positive people:** Positive people are not complainers; they find the good in everybody and every condition. These are the kind of people you should have around you. One way to find happiness is to be thankful for every little thing you have.

- **Find people with the same mindset and interests:** Staying around people who share common interests with you can be very inspiring. In your relationship with these people, you're not just on the receiving end, but you can also add value to their lives since you are interested in the same things. You can never feel alone when you are with them.

- **Surround yourself with successful people:** Earlier, we talked about happiness being contagious, but so is a success. The people you hang out with determining who you are or who you will be. When you begin to stay around people who have achieved great things, you gradually start to think, talk, and act like them. Soon, you will accomplish great things as well.

- **Be a good friend:** The people you are cutting off are described as harmful or toxic friends. It is hypocrisy to be cutting off people who do the exact things you do to others. Do you ever pay attention to the feelings of others? Do you constantly nag about other people's lives? Be a good friend if you need a good friend.

Letting Go of Negative People

This step is a tough decision to make. We find it hard to let go of the people we have loved. Maybe because of the time and energy we've invested for so many years to keep the relationship going. However, this step is essential to have the peace of mind you long for.

Below are some tips on how to get out of a destructive relationship:

- **Consider the positives of life without this person**: Sometimes, all we need do is think. Think about all the exciting and positive things you could do without this friend or partner in your life like the things you want to do, but you are restricted because of this person. Think about the positive turn your life would take if the relationship is ended. Your emotions could hinder your decision, so try hard to think with your head and not your heart.

- **Consider the fallout of saying goodbye**: You must take time to reflect on the consequences of saying goodbye.

Ending a relationship with one person could affect your relationship with others. Are you ready to lose anyone attached to you through this person? Are you strong enough to handle the heartbreak? How would the person react to this decision? These are some of the things you should reflect upon. Sit back and think about all the possible reactions of the person and how you would handle them. Take time to assess the after-effects of ending the relationship or of staying in it, and then you should choose.

- **Define what goodbye means**: For a relationship, define what goodbye means to you. Some relationships end with no form of communication at all, while others involve people still talking to one another at times with precaution. So how do you want yours to go? As explained earlier, you can't completely get rid of family members, because they are part of your existence, whether you like it or not. So, in cases like these, setting boundaries could be the best way out. For other people, you can either cut them off entirely or relate with them differently. In other words, you can decide how and when to talk to them, how they affect your emotional health, and what to condone from them. However, this time, you shouldn't allow them to hurt you, as you are in control.

- **Communicate your intention without blame**: Despite the pain these people have caused you, ending the relationship without any form of explanation isn't the right way to go about it. A simple statement to back up your decision will do. You can call this person, send them a letter, or meet up with them; either way, give them a reason. You don't have to blame anyone for your decision or concentrate on the person's imperfections.

- **Create a plan for a negative reaction**: Have a backup plan for any negative reactions in the future. You can discuss your decision with people who knew about your relationship with the individual, telling them about your reason for ending it without tarnishing the image of the person. So, in case of a bad or stressful situation, they will support you.

- **Accept that it can be a process**: Moving on from a relationship can take a while. For some, it can take years, while for others, it can take months. Whatever the case is, know that letting go is a process. Frequently, it can be so hard that some people try to build up the relationship again, only to worsen the situation. Acknowledge that moving on can take time, and you will be able to stand on your own eventually.

- **Allow yourself to grieve**: When you let go of someone that was close or dear to you, it is not unusual to grieve over them. You feel the pain, and the loss and your heart might ache, but do not discard it, for this is part of the healing process. When you allow yourself to grieve, the pain leaves sooner than you expect, and you can start all over again.

Your Quick Start Action Step:

1. Make a table of three columns. List names of people who have contributed positively to your life in the left column, a list of people who haven't added anything to your life in the middle column, and people who have contributed negatively to your life on the right.

2. Make another table of three columns. This time, make a list of people to whom you've contributed something on the left, people you've contributed nothing to their life in the middle, and people you have contributed negatively to their life on the right.

3. Write specific goals for how you intend to contribute positively to people around you.

4. Now write down a list of people you intend to cut from your life gradually.

Chapter 8: Freeing Your Mind from Worry, Anxiety, and Stress

Chapter 8: Freeing Your Mind from Worry, Anxiety, and Stress

For a significant part of our lives, we all struggle with mental clutter. We always feel like whatever happens; mental clutter is always present; something is continually running through our mind. It could be a new thing that is making us feel worried or disorganized; it might be a memory haunting us. Some days, it might be bearable, and other days, it might not. However, the feeling is always present.

The voices you hear in your head will never be still: You keep hearing your boss instructing you to get the reports ready by Friday, your son telling you not to forget about soccer practice on Saturday, or the voices of your parents reminding you to help them clean up the house this weekend.

We all have places to be every day, including the strenuous jobs we do daily at home or work. It might feel too intense, and turbulent thoughts may disturb our minds. A few of us may even hear voices echoing from past experiences.

Causes of Mental Clutter

Daily stress. The main reason a lot of people feel like life is overwhelming is that they are extremely stressed. The stress caused by physical clutter, information overload, and the limitless options needed for these things can set off a few mental health problems, such as depression, generalized anxiety, and panic attacks.

Add all these to the real concerns and worries in your life, and you might start to experience muscle pain, chest pain, sleep problems, intestinal disorders, frequent infections, headaches, and stomach disorders. This finding is according to the American Psychological Association and several studies that prove a link between physical problems and stress.

The moment life starts to become complicated and overwhelming. Our subconscious mind begins to seek escape options. Excess harmful exposure, an abundance of options, and excess input are likely to set off an unhealthy coping mechanism.

The paradox of choice. Concerning mental health, the freedom of choice (which is honored in free societies) may have a diminishing effect. The phrase "paradox of choice" was created by Barry Schwartz, a psychologist. According to Schwartz, when choices are abundant, it results in more paralysis, anxiety, dissatisfaction, and confusion. Additional decisions might result in better outcomes without necessarily making you happy.

Jeans are very popular. Try to buy a pair, and you will have to choose from several options that are available: skinny, vintage wash, baggy fit, button fly, boot cut, or wide leg. The thought of shopping is enough to stress you out.

Too much stuff. Most of our houses are packed with clothes that may never be worn, books that will never be read, gadgets that are never used, or toys that have never been touched. Then there are many unread messages on our computers, our phones keep giving us notifications like "insufficient storage space", and our desktop area is filled with clutter.

A reply must be sent to every text and email. The newest device or gadget must be bought. Everything seems serious and vital.

These demands make us always busy, occupied with irrelevant things, suppressing our emotions, and getting emotionless toward the people around us.

Often, we feel like decluttering is too time-consuming, and we would instead study new things and information. Eventually, all these activities will result in emotional and mental stress. While processing all the things we experience, we ruminate, we assess and get incredibly anxious.

The negativity bias. This bias refers to our inclination to respond to negative stimuli more strongly compared to positive stimuli. The neural activity produced by negative stimuli is higher compared to that created by positive stimuli of equal magnitude (in terms of sound and light). The brain also senses negative stimuli faster and easier than positive ones. "The brain is similar to Velcro for the negative experience; whereas, for positive experiences, it can be likened to Teflon." - Hanson.

Thus, how do negative stimuli affect your thoughts? It indicates that you are inclined to worry, overthink, and evaluate situations more negatively. You view challenges as particularly tricky and threats as extra threatening. There is a feeling of realness for every negative thought that filters into your mind, so you instantly accept it as reality. However, you do not live in a cave, going through near-death experiences every day. Although you might be inclined to view things negatively, you can choose to avoid accepting that inclination.

Meditation

Meditation is an age-old tradition that is believed to have originated in Hindu, Chinese, and Buddhist cultures. There are so many methods of practicing meditation, but a majority of these methods start with the same steps: Sitting peacefully, concentrating all your attention on breathing, and discarding all distractions.

The objective of meditation differs in the kind of medication practice and the desired result of the participant. However, for the purpose of this book, we recommend meditation as a kind of mind-training tool that also helps you control your thoughts; regardless of whether you are in the sitting position or not during meditation.

The positive effects of meditation eventually start to become evident in your daily life, helping you to stop over-thinking, controlling worry and resulting in a lot of health benefits, which you will discover as you read on.

The secret to having a positive outcome with meditation is to keep practicing.

By dedicating a part of your day to meditation, you will develop your skills and experience the eventual benefits on your emotional, mental, and physical health.

Let us start with the basic 10-minute meditation that you can start right now. It is uncomplicated and straightforward. It does not require any special equipment or clothing. The only thing you need is a quiet place and the dedication to follow through.

This type of meditation is a fundamental but effective 11-part process that can be used to develop the habit.

1. Choose a serene, peaceful environment for your meditation. Practice where the door can be shut, and you can be completely alone.

2. Choose a specific time of the day for your session. If you have started a deep breathing session, this can be used as an activator (and starting point) for your new meditation practice. You can also select another activator and meditate at a different time of the day.

3. Decide if you want to meditate by sitting on a pillow, a sofa, a chair or on the floor. Since you might fall asleep, try not to lean backward.

4. Get rid of every distraction, and switch off every digital gadget or other gadgets that may be noisy. Take your pet out of the room.

5. Fix a timer for 10 minutes.

6. Sit cross-legged or normally sit, either on a chair or a cushion placed on the floor. Maintain an erect spine, and place your hands softly over your lap.

7. Keep your eyes closed. But if you prefer to open them, do it while looking downward. Then inhale a few deep cleansing breaths using your nose. We advise taking three or four breaths at once.

8. Slowly become aware of your breathing. Take note of the air going in and out of your nostrils and the upward and downward movements of your abdomen. Do not force your breaths, but rather let them come spontaneously.

9. Concentrate on your breathing. You can also try to mentally picture the word "in" while you inhale and "out" while exhaling.

10. In the initial stages, you would be distracted by your thoughts. Each time you are distracted, let go of those thoughts gently and focus your attention back to the process of breathing.

11. Do not beat yourself up over distracting thoughts. Your monkey mind is merely trying to take control. Guide your mind back to concentrating all the attention on breathing. You might have to do this a few times in the beginning.

12. While all your concentration is on your breathing, you will likely be more aware of other sensations and perceptions, such as physical unease, emotions, or sounds. Just take note of the times you become aware of them and carefully focus your attention back to the sensational breathing.

Your aim is to progressively become aware of all sensations, thoughts, feelings, and emotions as they develop and fade away. Look at them as if you are only viewing them from a distance with no internal comments or judgment.

Instead of your mind taking charge and losing focus as soon as a distraction or thought occurs, eventually, you can control your mind at a maximum level and become skilled at redirecting focus back to where you are at that moment.

Initially, you might feel as if you are in a constant fight with your monkey mind. However, consistent practice means that there will be no need to redirect your thoughts always. Naturally, thoughts begin to fade away, and your brain becomes open to the limitless vastness and silence of merely being there. This moment is an intensely quiet and satisfying feeling.

Mindfulness

Gradual, deep, rhythmic breathing is one effective method of isolating negative thoughts and controlling your mind. This concentrated breathing activates the parasympathetic nervous system, causing muscle relaxation, a reduction in heart rate, normalized brain activity, and a quiet mind.

Deep breathing creates a connection between you and your body, taking your awareness away from your anxiety and silencing the internal conversations in your brain. Deep breathing results in physiological changes that are commonly called the "relaxation response".

If you practice a few minutes of abdominal breathing daily, you are developing a permanent habit that has been discovered to lower stress, clear your mind, and enhance the relaxation of the body and mind. This relaxation technique is based on many years of extensive research and testing. Try out the following steps:

1. Locate a comfortable place where you can comfortably concentrate without any distractions or interruptions.

2. Position yourself in a posture that is alert and relaxed with your back positioned straight.

3. Breath deeply and relax. You can choose to either leave your eyes open or closed. Continue inhaling and exhaling using slow, deep breaths.

4. With your eyes closed, let go of all your problems now as if you are dropping a heavy bag. Know that you are giving yourself this time to detach from external worries.

5. Next, concentrate on your breath. Become totally aware of your sensation of breathing.

6. Begin to count your breaths gently, starting from one and going up to ten, then beginning all over again. If you observe that you missed the sequence before getting to ten, then repeat the process, because this means that you were distracted.

7. Become deeply engrossed in your breathing. Begin to observe the sound, volume, speed, and warmth of your breath going in and out through your

nose.

8. Now, concentrate on the thoughts wandering through your mind, trying to divert your attention away from your breath. Observe them carefully. This step is the most important one.

9. Experience an increased sensation of peace within you as you continue to settle into breathing with more concentration. Take note of how it feels to be in the middle of the fleeting contents of awareness and what it feels like to let them fade away. Notice the calm awareness itself. As soon as you get to this relaxed awareness, you can choose to remain in that state for as long as you desire. Conclude the meditative session by opening your hands, stretching your hands, and standing up.

Your Quick Start Action Step:

1. Write down a list of things that cause you anxiety, worry, and mental stress, and write down why they do so.

2. Now, do a quick meditation or mindfulness practice as highlighted in the chapter

To learn more about freeing your mind from worry, anxiety, and stress, check out "Declutter Your Mind: How to Free Your Thoughts from Worry, Anxiety & Stress Using Mindfulness Techniques for Better Mental Clarity and to Simplify Your Life" by Marie S. Davenport in the online store.

Chapter 9: Decluttering in the Workplace

Chapter 9: Decluttering in the Workplace

Productivity is affected by a decluttered workplace, so clutter should be addressed. We will be discussing this issue in the following chapter.

Why is it Important to Achieve a Clutter-Free Workplace?

You are creating additional space. Office rentals do not come cheap. This option can take up a sizable portion of your business budget. Unfortunately, many businesses retain too much space for irrelevant storage that they do not even need. You should think about getting a document scanning device that will assist in sorting, scanning, and digitizing your files. Some companies also offer the service of shredding redundant documents after converting them to digital versions. There is an incredible method of creating additional space on cabinets, reducing the clutter in storage rooms, and creating significant extra space.

You can also reserve an area or room to store damaged hardware or obsolete equipment that is out of use. You can also make extra cash by recycling or selling outdated hardware that you no longer need. Just try not to allow these items to occupy unnecessary space.

Become organized. Chaos is one of the consequences of a cluttered workplace. You can make your business organized by taking away excess clutter. For example, do you need so many keyboards and mice on your desk? If you have multiple computers or pieces of equipment on one desk, you can create additional space by donating a few of your peripherals to another colleague. Alternatively, you can put up a new desk, or sell them for more money. By doing this, there is additional space on your desk for other relevant things, such as useful documents and letters that may need to be checked. You won't have to look around everywhere to find simple items.

There is no need to look through cabinets or request to borrow things or devices from other members of staff and no more interruptions caused by a disorganized workplace. You can completely concentrate on increasing your productivity in the workplace rather than tidying up the mess created by other people.

Make your working environment as comfortable as possible. Most people prefer working in a quiet and decluttered environment. The secret to increasing productivity is making your workspace free of any distractions or clutter. In addition to promoting positive energy among members of your staff, a well-organized office also makes it easier to work. For instance, you should try to achieve good lighting and use rooms that are soundproof to prevent audio interruptions from outside or nearby offices.

Additionally, decorations like paintings and plants have a calming and relaxing effect on your employees. It lowers their stress levels and uplifts their moods when they must carry out essential tasks.

Making a good impression on clients and new employees. Even if your office is comfortable enough for you and allows you to get the job done, if your office is disorganized, it might drive away customers, potential employees, and clients. To them, the place looks like a total disaster.

If you are concerned about making an excellent first impression, you must organize your office so that it does not look like a mess when an important person visits for a meeting.

In the business world, first impressions matter, so put in a lot of effort to reduce the clutter, organize your workplace, and train your employees to abide by these principles. So when a potential investor visits, there is a higher chance that they will provide funds for your business, rather than telling their friends not to do business with you.

Steps to Declutter Your Workplace

1. Take inventory: Before you begin the process of decluttering your desk, take some time, and make an inventory of your current arrangements. Inspect your desk and its surroundings. Decide on the areas that are included in your workspace that require your attention. These might consist of filing storage, your desk, or anything related to your work that is stored close. Consider also those that are probably in another location or room. Observe the degree of clutter and the overall activity. Get a proper review of what you must handle. Taking physical or mental notes can help you do this.

2. Assess and imagine: Reflect on the periods spent at your desk or workplace and your habits. Are you working from home and all you do is get out of bed, sit on your desk, and check your emails while gobbling breakfast down? Have you fixed your working hours, regardless of whether you are on your desk or not? Do you do things that are not related to work in your area?

Make notes of these things, and assess how beneficial your current habits are to you or if you may need to make modifications to some of them. Imagine your ideal workspace and desk habits. Continue to reflect on this vision in your mind, and allow it to determine your decisions as you move through further steps.

3. Clear up: Take everything away from your desk, and clear out every other storage unit containing your work materials. This step means every single item, including the tiny pictures and post-it notes on your computer. While you are doing this, you can sort everything to these four groups: 1. papers, 2. books, 3. mementos (items such as pictures that hold memories for you), and 4. other (a collection of other things that do not fit into any group). However, you can create as many subgroups as you like.

4. Clean: Take the bold step, and clean your computer screen, desk, and every other thing. There is a high probability that insects and dirt might have gathered over time, and you may have never had the opportunity to clean your workspace meticulously. There is no better time than now. You might be discouraged initially, but keep in mind that it is more enjoyable to work in an environment that's clean and organized.

5. Change the arrangements: Since everything is clean and empty, consider how beneficial your present arrangement is. You might want to arrange your computer or your desk completely, or perhaps a few of your filing cabinets would be more useful om another position. This opportunity is the best time to make these modifications.

6. Declutter: Now, you must deal with those items you previously placed in those four groups. Look through them in that order, and decide if each object creates a feeling of happiness. Also analyze whether they are supposed to be in your workspace and, most importantly, whether they are vital to your work.

7. Organize: Next, it is time to return the items you would like to keep on your desk and in other storage units. While doing so, keep similar items together, and store a large number of the items in storage units and drawers. Make an effort to keep your desk and other work surfaces as clear as they can be. Additionally, consider how many times you use objects and designate a location for them. What you are trying to achieve is to position all your items in a particular area. This way, you know where everything is located, and it will be easier to return items quickly after each use.

8. Discard: Now that your desk and surrounding areas have been organized, the next thing to do is to deal with those items that do not evoke a positive emotion. Decide on which items to discard, recycle, donate, or return. For instance, borrowed books that must be returned to a friend, colleague, or the library. Then make plans to do just that.

9. Develop new habits: Reflect on your initial objective, and decide whether you want to develop new habits in your personal life and workplace and how to go about it. Additionally, for your desk and workplace to remain decluttered, ensure that you return all items to their particular spaces each day before leaving your workplace.

Your Quick Start Action Step:

1. Assess how disorganized your office desk is.

2. Picture how you want it to look.

3. Now, write the process you intend to follow to get it decluttered, following the steps listed in this chapter.

Chapter 10: Freeing Yourself from Digital Distractions and Clutter

Chapter 10: Freeing Yourself from Digital Distractions and Clutter

Digital clutter reduces the efficiency of the storage capacity of your computer, limiting the storage of your personal data and files. This buildup is why it is necessary to routinely digital declutter to improve the efficiency of your computer. Digital clutter is also a large and mostly unseen killer of productivity. The way you arrange your file folders, browser, and your desktop can easily distract and reduce your productivity. You may not realize how much you are being affected by clutter if your set-up remains unchanged. Distractions such as social media also add to clutter in life and must be dealt with appropriately.

Why It's Important to Deal with Digital Clutter and Distractions

1. **To develop better critical thinking skills:** The brain is likely to become dull and could be overloaded with information

when too much time is spent with technology. It is crucial to distance yourself from this distraction to dive into fresh ideas. These concepts require the use of critical thinking skills that will be hard to develop if you rely too much on technology.

2. **To learn essential skill sets:** Although you might understand a procedure by watching a video, you will never really learn it unless you try it on your own. This action requires you to leave the virtual world and enter into the physical world for actual results. Although technology is a great learning tool, using it to consume content until you get information overload can be distracting. True learning is achieved through practice. You do not only attain knowledge, but you also genuinely learn additional skills when you reduce digital clutter.

3. **To reconnect with or discover new passions:** Digital decluttering helps to

increase your free time, allowing you to reconnect to old goals and dreams or to form new ones. Reducing digital clutter will enable you to pursue activities such as run a marathon, further your education, write a book, or learn an instrument.

4. **To maintain good vision**: Staring at the screen for an extended period can damage the eyes. To maintain good vision, awareness of this is necessary to reduce the time spent on digital activities.

5. **To allow for time to engage the senses:** Digital decluttering will also enable you to have more time to interact with the real world, leading you to enjoy your physical environment. It requires you to cook a meal from scratch, go for a walk, talk to a friend, and learn through experiences.

6. **To stay in shape:** Reducing digital clutter also leads to you taking better care of yourself. Although technologies

accurately monitor and time your workout sessions, endeavor that the technology is running in the background. Thirty minutes to an hour is all you need for a good workout per day. Refraining from technology for that period should be done to care for yourself. With time, you begin to realize that the longer you care for your body, the less you'll rely on technology.

7. **To reconnect with or discover new passions:** Digital decluttering helps you take more interest in the people present in your life. Spending more time with those you love makes it easier for you to stay away from the virtual world.

8. **To become more active socially:** Staying away from the virtual world gets you more opportunities for social activities. This exposure helps improve your interaction with others. This change also leads to others becoming more interesting to you **as a result.**

9. **To allow for more reading time:** Reading improves your communication skills as well as your writing skills. Reading informs and entertains you. Using less technology will enable you to access all of that. Although you can read books on a tablet, the attraction of paper and the weight of a book is difficult to replace. Do not miss out on that by replacing it with mindless scrolling on social media.

10. **To grow in marketability:** Taking advantage of the benefits listed above helps you become more valuable and marketable as an individual, personally, and professionally. It makes you more socially attractive and appealing to others. Also, you have an advantage with potential employers over other job seekers.

How to Digital Declutter

1. Declutter your digital documents.

- Thoroughly check all your documents, deleting those that are no longer needed.

- Do not allow the just-in-case syndrome to occur, as you do not need notes from an outdated project, nor do you need the old essays.

- Peradventure you have many files, arrange them according to their dates and start with the documents that are the oldest. To prevent yourself from getting tired, divide the process into chunks.

2. Organize and delete images.

    - Your pictures should be arranged in folders by event or date.

    - The pictures should be kept in a cloud drive, such as DropBox or OneDrive, to ensure that you do not need to store them on your computer.

- Photos that are either unimportant or of poor quality should be deleted.

3. Clear out your downloads.

    - If you have never cleaned your download folder, it probably takes up a lot of space on your computer.

    - To prevent you from being overwhelmed, sort your files according to date, and delete them in bits.

    - All the contents in your download folder can be deleted if your important files have already been backed up.

4. Clean up your bookmarks.

    - Deleting your bookmarks also helps you to streamline your browser window.

    - Bookmarks that aren't needed should be deleted, and those that are necessary can be saved with apps such as Pocket or Evernote.

5. Make a zen desktop.

- As a clean desk also allows one to be more focused and productive, so does having a clean desktop.

- Shortcuts of apps should be removed, and folders and files on the desktop should also be cleaned up.

- Your desktop interface should be made tidier.

- Do not forget to conceal the default taskbar.

6. Delete rarely used accounts.

    - Deletion of unnecessary and rarely used accounts helps to prevent time-wasting and reduce the number of passwords to remember.

    - Some apps are created to provide a list of sites usually used and how difficult it is to delete your account on each site.

7. Unsubscribe from email lists/newsletters.

- Refrain from thinking that deals and newsletters will be needed later, as they won't be.

- Online shopping deals are the best to unsubscribe from, as they are regular and fill up your inbox.

- If it is necessary to get a newsletter from a particular site, change your email preference to get fewer newsletters. A link is usually placed at the bottom of the newsletters to change your email preferences (although some only offer to unsubscribe).

- For a week or two, open all newsletters you get, and edit your email preferences; this prevents you from being overwhelmed going through your inbox at once.

8. Make sure to defrag/clean your disk.

- This step should be done consistently. If you don't currently do this, check your computer's disk clean options in your computer's settings, and do it immediately. You can find out where it is located on your computer if you do not already know, or ask help from a tech expert.

- Defragging may be scheduled automatically or manually, depending on your OS.

- Third-party apps, such as Disk Space Fan, can also be used.

9. Use automated inbox sorting.

    - Your inbox can be programmed to sort your incoming emails if you are making use of Gmail.

    - Some apps from a third party can also assist you in sorting your inbox.

10. Unfriend, unfollow, and in general, clean out your social newsfeeds.

    - You only get relevant updates when you unfollow people on Twitter. This option enables you to get important news updates on Twitter, be it related to work or personal news. You can also mute anyone you wish to on your Twitter feed.

You will be able to have better access to essential posts on your newsfeed when you unfriend irrelevant people on Facebook. This change will help you to be up-to-date on the activities of your loved ones without spending too much time on the site. Scroll through your list of liked pages and friends and start unfriending.

Your Quick Start Action Step:

1. Write down the ten things that distract you digitally, starting from most to least distracting.

2. Write down how controlling the distractions you get from these gadgets will be beneficial to you.

3. Write down the specific steps you'll take in decluttering your digital life, including

a timeframe for each step.

Chapter 11: The Simple Lifestyle

Chapter 11: The Simple Lifestyle

Living life in a simple manner makes life easier. People assume that genuinely living a happy life requires status, shopping for expensive items, gossiping, or other forms of drama, but it only results in dissatisfaction. With a lifestyle that allows you to experience reduced stress and a more relaxed mind, these are some of the advantages of a simple life, depending on the choices you make.

The Keys to Living a Simple Life include:

- **Defining your needs:** Once you understand your needs, you will also realize the things you do not need. Your life naturally becomes simpler.

- **Being intentional:** A powerful way of living your life is by intentional acting and thinking. Once you question yourself on the intentions behind whatever you do, you are actively controlling your life.

- **Understanding your control:** You can only make changes to things within your sphere of influence. You can live a simple life only if you act on things you can control, leaving the things that are not in your control.

Why It's Important to Aim for a Simple Lifestyle

1. **Conscious consumption:** You begin conscious consumption to stop your attachment to addictive use. Living a simple life makes you aware of your spending choices. This mindset makes anything you purchase more valuable. Your awareness of the environmental impact of the consumable goods and the way it sustains a living becomes greater. You make your purchases wisely considering all necessary options.

2. **Achieve more with less:** Living a simple life allows you to have fewer worries, less energy drain, and fewer distractions. You begin to think more

explicit, and your life becomes gently paced. You allow more time to understand yourself, which helps you realize and achieve your goals in life. Your energy becomes more focused on fewer and more important goals, which generates better results.

3. **A satisfying lifestyle becomes your priority:** Instead of concentrating on getting more material things, you begin to prioritize for a simpler lifestyle. You start to focus on things that are important to you and not on what the media or other people say. Your lifestyle should be designed to be as meaningful and thoughtful as possible in order to fulfill your inner being.

4. **Your self-worth is no longer connected to the stuff you have accumulated:** You start to take into account more of your self-esteem, and your inspiration for jumping out of bed every morning is not related to the things

you acquire. Your soul cannot be satisfied with addictive consumption. You begin to determine the motives that drove you to buy many things and instead focus more on your self-worth.

5. **You now value the gift of time:** Time is seen as a valuable commodity that is better spent by an individual in a more meaningful and relaxed manner. Instead of having a large home that takes up your time with cleaning, repairing, and maintenance, you should buy a smaller home that saves you energy and time. Time wasters such as watching TV should also be reduced to get a greater sense of value for your time, and you should only work hours befitting your improved lifestyle.

6. **The law of diminishing returns:** The pleasure you derive from experience or having more of something diminishes over time. The first surge of enjoyment felt when purchasing a new item slowly

reduces with constant exposure. This shift is usually observed in children filled with excitement at the first experience of owning a toy, but the novelty wears off quickly. Purchasing more things to improve your well-being is not a good long term solution for a more satisfying life.

7. **Your stuff no longer demands your attention:** The things that fill your home continually demands your attention. Energy and time are needed to purchase them in the first place. Once they get into your homes, you are to decide if they should be cleaned, rearranged, repaired, stored, insured, used, not used, taken out, thought about again, put away, or reorganized into better storage. You also need to decide sometime in the future if you wish to give them away, throw them out, or keep them. This situation leads to a lot of worrying, thinking, energy, and time being channeled on your things,

which prevents you from living a simpler lifestyle.

8. **Reduces money stress:** Your money stress is reduced when you live in a smaller but more manageable house that satisfies your needs and helps you save a lot of money. You no longer have to worry about the changes in the mortgage interest rates, and you also spend less money on furniture, cleaning products, heating and cooling, decorations, and things that conform to your finite storage capacity. The family also becomes closer emotionally and physically in a smaller but cozy home.

Minimalist Living

Minimalism is a means of you discovering freedom. This statement could mean freedom from depression, from being overwhelmed, feeling guilty, being worried, or freedom from the consumer culture, which has been made to govern our lives. This is real freedom.

Having material things is not necessarily a bad

thing. The problem is that we tend to give a great deal of meaning to our things, often abandoning our passions, personal growth, health, relationships, and our desire to impact others positively. Do you wish to own a big house or brand new car, or do you desire to have a successful career or to raise a family? Choosing the former is relatively not a problem as long as these things really mean something to you. Minimalism simply helps you make your decisions intentionally.

Minimalist living involves a whole new lifestyle. And although having a clutter-free environment is a significant part of it, it includes so much more. Minimalist living also consists in observing the way you spend your money, time, and even how you think.

Living a minimal lifestyle helps you attain happiness, which is what everyone wishes for, right? Happiness is determined by life itself and not by the things we acquire in life. It is therefore up to you to decide what you need and what is unnecessary in your life.

How to Maintain a Simple Lifestyle

1. **Be kind:** You will not go far in life if the majority does not like you.

2. **Don't criticize:** Whenever you wish to criticize anyone, do not forget that every person does not have access to things you do. Although it is easy to criticize, it is difficult for you to identify if you are criticizing because of boredom, fear, or jealousy.

3. **Don't expect too much:** It is impossible to have your way in all things. It will always seem like something is missing. The point at which you begin to rely on your emotions is the moment you begin to make unfounded assumptions. This attitude makes you lose. Always expect the best and the worst at the same time.

4. **Be present:** Feel the pain while you are exercising. Do not use music to silence it, nor should you ignore the pain. Always live in the moment. You should always be

aware of everything you do, feel, and tell yourself. Learn to stay strong through it. Stop making excuses whenever you are feeling discomfort. Use everything you can to learn this.

5. **Dealing with idiots, arrogance, and the like:** We live in an ecosystem of largely crazy individuals. Some people out there wake up and walk in the same crap daily, rather than stepping around it or clearing it from their lane. They castigate everyone aside from themselves.

6. **Tell yourself a different story:** When whatever's being said does not sit well with you, start your own discourse.

7. **Redefine everything in your life:** Odds are you've heard all sorts of lies about being successful, influential, and living the best life. Being successful has been predefined as finishing college, landing a great job, getting a good car, having a wonderful body, etc. These things are necessarily not equivalent to

real success for everyone, and they do not need to be. The American Dream might play out well for others but not work for you.

Redefine success for yourself: Reevaluate the meaning of life to you. Reexamine the beliefs that were ingrained in you to make you follow someone else's vision and keep you playing it safe in life. Immediately after you find out what you really want, go out and make it happen.

8. **Ask why:** Question yourself on why you do the things you do. If getting a relevant answer becomes a problem for you, then you should likely not do it. For instance, I had a Facebook account and had about 700 friends, with around 10 of them being my actual friends. Still, I kept on logging onto this virtual world for no substantial reason. I would monitor the lives of others and concentrate on them rather than focus on myself, my work, and my real friends. Bring clarity to the reasons

you do the things you do and if there is a genuine intent to back it. Question yourself about ways you can be better.

9. **Focus on you:** Stop fixating and getting bothered about how other people live their lives. Life gets better when you learn to close off the outside noise and concentrate more on yourself.

Your Quick Start Action Step:

1. Write down the three most crucial things that you want your life to revolve around.

2. Analyze your life as it is. Jot down what you do daily, who you spend your time with, what your expenses are, what your place of abode is, and every other thing you can think of. How do they all back your values, and how do they work with these values?

3. Go over everything you wrote down, and eliminate what does not back your values and what you do not want in your happier life. Discard the regret and liabilities, and

concentrate on the things that make you happy.

4. Write out what you would like to include in your life to better back your values. In what ways are they suitable for your new life? This task can be more straightforward if done on a computer, as you can simply move things around.

5. Take note of a minute thing you can do to be a step closer to your happier and more comfortable life. Transform your diet one meal at a time. Leave a group that's not contributing to your development anymore. Begin to walk more. Remain around people that use up your energy less. Clear a cluttered area in your life, whether it be emotionally or physically.

6. Every time you take a step regarding your new life, pause and contemplate how you feel. Is it benefiting you or do you need to change something about it?

1. Decide to dwell intimately with your brand new life daily, and keep cultivating

new habits

2. Carry out an action that backs up your values. You can do this activity every day, and ensure you take time to observe how it feels inside. As you adhere to the process, these small things would eventually add up in helping you become a better version of yourself.

Bonus Chapter: Planning Family Recreational Activities

Bonus Chapter: Planning Family Recreational Activities

An increasing number of employees do not even use their vacation leave anymore. Tasks like work, school, screen time, extracurricular activities, and daily routines draw families in separate directions. Coming together can be like herding cats. Arranging a calendar must be deliberate, and it depends on the unity and engagement of all the members of the family.

Decluttering your life is more than arranging and clearing your physical space. It needs a deliberate technique to plan your time and set up activities with your family. Decluttering one's life also makes room for more fun and recreation. It has been proven that more recreation time reduces stress, which we want to reduce or eliminate, whenever possible. New research4).

Why It's Important to Plan for Recreational Activities

_____

- **Everyone needs a break:** The daily routine burns us out, and most times, a vacation is one of the ways to get away and ignore work and a tight schedule. A vacation can help you unwind and forget about the stress of your daily life, and it should be cheerful and fun. When you take a vacation, you come back invigorated, and you become a better employee, a better spouse, and a better parent.

- **Lasting memories:** Kids enjoy going through scrapbooks where your memories of your family vacation are documented. They will discuss their adventures, such as the things they've seen and the fun they had on the leaves. These are memories they will share with their children someday, and this is important. Your kids will know that you loved being with them and spending time with them through these family vacations.

- **Open your eyes:** Going on vacation with your kids will open them up to new people and new cultures, which is a good thing. Even if you do not go outside of your home country, your children can learn about the local cuisines from you, the history of the region, and learn about locations and activities. Help them understand that the world is their classroom.

- **Reconnect:** Vacations strengthen relationships and family ties. Carrying out activities that are not part of what you usually do and leaving your comfort zone will help strengthen you as an individual and your family.

- **It's about time:** A vacation is us time, with no emails to read, laundry to fold, or bathrooms to scrub. You can concentrate on each other doing whatever you want to, even if it's just lying on the beach and watching your kids play in the sand. Does that not sound great?

Steps for Planning a Recreational Activity

1. Get a calendar for the period you want to plan for. It is excellent to have it printed out. I recommended planning for the future; if possible, at least, prepare for a month. The real advantage of this is seen when you plan for a whole season (about 3-6 months out). This approach works because taking an extensive view of your family responsibilities and reviewing your checklist will ensure your calendar is not packed. This assessment leaves room for flexibility and increases the probability that your family will do all the fun things they have planned.

2. Write out all your family's already planned responsibilities:

   - Birthday parties. If a birthday party you just cannot miss is coming up, you can modestly buzz the parents and ask when they're planning the party, so you do not miss it).

   - Church events

- Sports practices and games
- Planned travel/vacations
- Out of town guest visits

3. Take inventory of your family's rhythms, personality needs, etc.:

   - Do your kids need to nap?
   - What are your kids' bedtimes?
   - What is your budget?
   - When do you need to do your grocery shopping or do laundry?
   - Are there any special adult events coming up?
   - What balance do you want between scheduled activities and free play?
   - What are the pockets of time you have?

4. Let Google be your friend. You can even check Facebook for where and when the best adventures are happening.

- Major special events (something that happens only once in a year)
- Special events for the local area (annual events, a special parade, etc.)
- Special events for a venue
- Seasonal (Christmas lights, Easter eggs, strawberry picking season, fall festivals)
- A mix of activities
    - Day-long trips
    - Half-day trips
    - Easy and quick trips (1-2 hours)
    - City stuff
    - Fairs and festivals
    - Amusement parks
    - Parks and playgrounds
    - Museums
    - Nature centers

- Indoor activities
- Outdoor activities

5. Create a bucket list of family fun activities and set it up:

   - Include the whole family in this process. Acknowledge the desires and needs of everyone in the family.

   - Arrange in order of priority, so you do not miss an activity or event.

6. Put the planned-out draft of activities into the fun schedule of your family. Don't try to fit everything in (it won't work!).

7. Ensure there's room for flexibility in your schedule. Be mindful of the activities that only occur once in a year or a season and the ones that are "Plug and Play", which can be plugged in anywhere.

   - Put in backup days for the vital activities.

   - If there's rain, what can be moved around?

- If any unplanned things occur, how can these opportunities be fit in?

- What if someone gets sick?

8. Build-in downtimes:

    - Weekly downtime

    - Monthly downtime. Designate at least one weekend where you are not all that busy. This approach doesn't mean you can't schedule anything, but that not every weekend can be a comprehensive trip to Six Flags or any amusement park.

9. Look into creating more special days aside from weekends. If you can manipulate your work schedule to take time off during the week, this will boost your family's fun plan. I make time during the week sometimes (because there are fewer people) to carry out activities like:

    - Checking out the tulip fields or sunflower fields

- Doing something special like going to an amusement park or a special beach

- Strawberry picking

10. Divide and conquer. You all do not have to go for everything as a family. Let yourself have some adult time, and bring a trustworthy adult along.

Your Quick Start Action Step:

Refer to the section "Steps on planning a recreational activity", and plan the steps discussed.

Conclusion

Thank you again for owning this book!

Decluttering your life can be a natural process that could lead you to a better and healthier lifestyle. It may require daily, time-to-time consciousness of your environment, dwelling, and state of mind. But achieving it is definitely doable, especially if it meets your personal goals.

Without intervention, your workplace and home would sway from place to place, becoming chaotic in pursuit of distractions. When you refuse to take care of your clutter, your being and dwelling will remain chaotic. Due to this, your life experiences will be variable and utterly reliant on the haphazard nature of things.

The chaos experienced in diverse aspects of your life depicts the annoying truth that many of the current systems are not under our deliberate control. To make matters worse, this chaos feels very concrete and robust, and they have an intense effect on our capacity and view of our surroundings.

In spite of all this, let the paralyzing feeling brought about by clutter go.

Even if your subconscious mind doesn't let you have total control over your nature, you have the power to handle many of them. You still can adjust so that you can control your clutter-developing tendencies.

Contained throughout this book is a comprehensive collection of insights and tools for decluttering your life. Thus, this book has provided you with tips that you could apply to the various facets of your life to achieve beneficial results for your lifestyle and general well being. These techniques would not only improve your life and reduce your stress levels but also give you that peace of mind.

Any necessary process requires patience, but the outcome is always worth it. However, before you start making any life-changing decisions, remember the importance of changing your mindset first. The truth is that we have varied mindsets at various times. Mindset is the outstanding shared characteristic successful people have. They have the correct attitude towards decluttering.

As you assess your fundamental values, you can then devise a plan for your decisions and actions. By doing so, you don't give yourself reasons to overthink and even worry.

Once your life priorities are clear, you do not squander your time on things that will cause you to regret or give you mental distress in the future.

You set the stage for targeted action and self-esteem that keeps you invigorated when your goals are established on your priorities and values.

When you set out and live your zeal, you saturate your goals with credibility, joy, and purpose with little or no room for pessimism.

By being more present and attentive in your relationships, you avoid most of the discord that comes with communicating with them. This step also reduces the emotional suffering that will come about and then maximizing contentment with the relationship.

By keeping your home and digital world clean, arranged, and streamlined, you take away distractions that prevent you from reaching your goals, priorities, and values.

By deciding to reduce your chores and obligations, you decrease your stress, hence allowing more time to be in the moment and to be more mindful of life.

When you concentrate on the job at hand at home and engage yourself into these decluttering endeavors, you fix the clutter in your dwelling to synchronize with the activity, promoting a sensation of great happiness and deep satisfaction. As you deal with procrastination and swiftly take the fundamental steps, you sidestep the tension that accompanies procrastinating and finish off the tasks.

By being attentive to the daily activities of life, from regular dishwashing to working out, you erase your mind out of everything else except on what is important - the present.

Outline your fundamental values, life preferences, and goals. When you have these personalized structures in place, it will be easier for you to ascertain where you have the most upsetting clutter and how you want to handle it.

All the practices stated in this book can be utilized for a brief amount of time daily. The outcome of these practices will help you with complicated ventures, such as bettering the organization of your home, time, family, and relationship, and discovering your passion or defeating the past.

Keep a journal where you write down the declutter practices you carry out and the changes seen in your life as a result. By tracking your actions and the outcomes, you'll feel encouraged to continue with your decluttering exercise.

Decluttering is a lifelong process that pays great rewards that can markedly affect your quality of life. The lesser time spent with meddlesome clutter in your life, the additional time you'll have to savor the present moment.

You have what it takes to achieve the lifestyle

that you deserve and fix the things that clutter your life, so take charge now. Start now with the most substantial clutter in your life to begin this process today.

Thank you and best of luck!

References

Decluttering Doesn't Work | The Minimalists. (2019). Retrieved from https://www.theminimalists.com/decluttering/

News, A. (2019). Einstein Was Right: Clutter Is Good. Retrieved from https://abcnews.go.com/Technology/tidy-messy-environment-impact-decisions-behavior-study/story?id=19909678

Liu, J., Smeesters, D., & Trampe, D. (2012). RETRACTED: Effects of Messiness on Preferences for Simplicity. Journal Of Consumer Research, 39(1), 199-214. doi: 10.1086/662139

Hoarding Disorders UK (2019). Retrieved from https://hoardingdisordersuk.org/wp-content/uploads/2014/01/clutter-image-ratings.pdf

5 Surprising Reasons Why Spring Cleaning is Good for You [LIST] - Goodnet. (2019). Retrieved from https://www.goodnet.org/articles/5-surprising-

reasons-spring-cleaning-good-for-you-list

Time Off and Vacation Usage. (2019). Retrieved from https://www.ustravel.org/toolkit/time-and-vacation-usage

Green, M., & Rosenfeld, L. (2014). Breathing Room: Open Your Heart by Decluttering Your Home. Simon and Schuster.

Johnson, B. (2013). Zero waste home: The ultimate guide to simplifying your life by reducing your waste. Simon and Schuster.

Desmarais, R. (2016). Time for spring cleaning and decluttering? But what about books?. The Deakin Review of Children's Literature, 5(4).

Harriet, S. (2005). Unclutter your life: is clutter creating chaos for you? Learn simple ways to declutter your home. IDEA Fitness Journal, 2(2), 94-96.

Bigelow, D. (2014). Clear the Clutter, Find Happiness: One-Minute Tips for Decluttering and Refreshing Your Home and Your Life.

Williamson, G. A. (2017). The Home

Decluttering Diet: Organize Your Way to a Clean and Lean House.

Fitzmartin, C. (2003). Home with Fun: Ten Steps to Turn Your Home Into a Fun Place to Live!. iUniverse.

www.ingramcontent.com/pod-product-compliance
Lightning Source LLC
Chambersburg PA
CBHW071237070526
44583CB00017B/2224